LORD
Send a Revival

CLARENCE SEXTON

FIRST EDITION
COPYRIGHT
JULY 2002

CROWN
PUBLICATIONS
Royal Reading

1700 BEAVER CREEK DRIVE
POWELL, TENNESSEE ❖ 37849
1-877 AT CROWN
www.FaithfortheFamily.com

SUNDAY SCHOOL SERIES

LORD, SEND A REVIVAL
Copyright © 2002
Crown Publications
Powell, Tennessee 37849
ISBN: 1-58981-106-2
Layout and design by Stephen Troell
Cover painting by Dylan Saunders, 2000

Printed in the United States of America

Dedication

his book is affectionately dedicated to Dr. Lee Roberson.

Dr. Roberson is the most Christ-like man I know. He truly walks with God. Throughout his life, he has allowed the Lord to use him in a miraculous way.

He is a New Testament pioneer having blazed a trail which untold thousands have followed. May God raise up a generation of preachers with the fire and compassion of Lee Roberson. Everything God has given me to do in the ministry has Dr. Roberson's handprint on it.

Clarence Sexton

Acts 5:42

Contents

THE KIND OF REVIVAL WE NEED

⇥ C·H· SPURGEON ⇤

We need a work of the Holy Spirit of a supernatural kind, putting power into the preaching of the Word, inspiring all believers with heavenly energy, and solemnly affecting the hearts of the careless, so that they turn to God and live. We would not be drunk with the wine of carnal excitement, but we would be filled with the Spirit. We would behold the fire descending from heaven in answer to the effectual fervent prayers of righteous men. Can we not entreat the Lord our God to make bare His holy arm in the eyes of all the people in this day of declension and vanity?

OLD-FASHIONED DOCTRINE

We want a revival of old-fashioned doctrine. I know not a single doctrine which is not at this hour studiously undermined by those who ought to be its defenders. There is not a truth that is precious to the soul which is not now denied by those whose profession it is to proclaim it. To me it is clear that we need a revival of old-fashioned gospel preaching like that of Whitefield and Wesley.

The Scriptures must be made the infallible foundation of all teaching; the ruin, redemption and regeneration of mankind must be set forth in unmistakable terms.

PERSONAL GODLINESS

Urgently do we need a revival of personal godliness. This is, indeed, the secret of church prosperity. When individuals fall from their steadfastness, the church is tossed to and fro; when personal faith is steadfast, the church abides true to her Lord. It is upon the truly godly and spiritual that the future of religion depends in the hand of God. Oh, for more truly holy men, quickened and filled with the Holy Spirit, consecrated to the Lord and sanctified by His truth.

Brethren, we must each one live if the church is to be alive; we must live unto God if we expect to see the pleasure of the Lord prospering in our hands. Sanctified men are the salt of society and the saviours of the race.

Domestic Religion

We deeply want a revival of domestic religion. The Christian family was the bulwark of godliness in the days of the puritans, but in these evil times hundreds of families of so-called Christians have no family worship, no restraint upon growing sons, and no wholesome instruction or discipline. How can we hope to see the kingdom of our Lord advance when His own disciples do not teach His gospel to their own children?

Oh, Christian men and women, be thorough in what you do and know and teach! Let your families be trained in the fear of God and be yourselves "holiness unto the Lord"; so shall you stand like a rock amid the surging waves of error and ungodliness which rage around us.

Vigorous, Consecrated Strength

We want also a revival of vigorous, consecrated strength. I have pleaded for true piety; I now beg for one of the highest results of it. We need saints. We need gracious minds trained to a high form of spiritual life by much converse with God in solitude.

Saints acquire nobility from their constant resort to the place where the Lord meets with them. There they also acquire that power in prayer which we so greatly need. Oh, that we had more men like John Knox, whose prayers were more terrible to Queen Mary than 10,000 men! Oh, that we had more Elijahs by whose faith the windows of heavens should be shut or opened!

This power comes not by a sudden effort; it is the outcome of a life devoted to the God of Israel! If our life is all in public, it will be a frothy, vapoury ineffectual existence; but if we hold high converse with God in secret, we shall be mighty for good. He that is a prince with God will take high rank with men, after the true measure of nobility.

Beware of being a lean-to; endeavour to rest on your own walls of real faith in the Lord Jesus. May none of us fall into a mean, poverty-stricken dependence on man! We want among us believers like those solid, substantial family mansions which stand from generation to generation as landmarks of the country; no lath-and-plaster fabrics, but edifices solidly constructed to bear all weathers, and defy time itself.

Given a host of men who are steadfast, immovable, always abounding in the work of the Lord, the glory of God's grace will be clearly manifested, not only in them, but in those round about them. The Lord send us a revival of consecrated strength, and heavenly energy!

Preach by your hands if you cannot preach by your tongues. When our church members show the fruits of true godliness, we shall soon have inquiries for the tree which bears such a crop.

Oh the coming together of the saints is the first part of Pentecost, and the ingathering of sinners is the second. It began with "only a prayer meeting," but it ended with a grand baptism of thousands of converts. Oh that the prayers of believers may act as lode stones to sinners! Oh that every gathering of faithful men might be a lure to attract others to Jesus! May many souls fly to Him because they see others speeding in that direction.

"Lord, we turn from these poor foolish procrastinators to Thyself, and we plead for them with Thine all-wise and gracious spirit! Lord, turn them and they shall be turned! By their conversion, pray that a true revival has commenced tonight! Let it spread through all our households, and then run from church to church till the whole of Christendom shall be ablaze with a heaven-descended fire!"

Yours very truly

C. H. Spurgeon

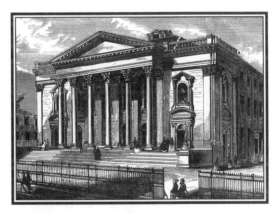

SPURGEON'S METROPOLITAN TABERNACLE
LONDON, ENGLAND

*"The burden which Habakkuk
the prophet did see."*

Habakkuk 1:1

The Need of the Hour is a Man with a "Burden". Must have the need, but do not overlay it.

Jer 29:13

II Chronicl 7:14

A Man With a Burden

I n this book of the Bible, we meet a man with a burden for God to do what only He could do. The book of Habakkuk is one of the twelve books found in the Old Testament that are referred to as the Minor Prophets. The term "minor" relates to the length of this book, not to the message. In every book of the Bible there is a major message. In this book of Habakkuk, we find the major message of all the Word of God, *"The just shall live by his faith"* (Habakkuk 2:4). This means no matter what our circumstances may be, we can be victorious through faith in the Lord Jesus Christ. We have a changeless God who is *"the same yesterday, and to day, and for ever"* (Hebrews 13:8).

Habakkuk lived on the eve of the captivity of his nation. In a sense, his day was the "day before destruction." The Babylonians were about to come down upon the nation of Judah, the Southern Kingdom, and destroy it. They were going to take the people of God captive to the land of Babylon. The temple of

[handwritten: What causes a burden? 1. The Spirit of God 2. The Situation by The Word]

the Lord would be ransacked and destroyed. This man of God, Habakkuk, was called to serve the Lord on the eve of this destruction. He was a contemporary of Jeremiah. They both served under the wicked reign of King Jehoiakim, who turned his back upon the Lord and upon the Word of God. In an age of wickedness, with the judgment of God at hand, Habakkuk sought the Lord.

> *No one is ever greatly used of God who does not have a burden.*

In this book of Habakkuk, we are listening to a conversation that a man had with God. God has recorded Habakkuk's conversation so that all might hear and heed. In this conversation we find many things that will move our hearts.

The Bible says in Habakkuk 1:1, *"The burden which Habakkuk the prophet did see."*

Notice in the very beginning that this prophet was a man with a burden. No one is ever greatly used of God who does not have a burden. *[handwritten: Transitional Sentence]*

We should possess a burden to be right with God. We need a burden for those in our homes to know the Lord Jesus Christ as Savior. We need a burden for the people of our cities to know the Lord. We need a burden for our churches to be the kind of churches that obey God's will. We need a burden for our nation to turn to the Lord. This man's burden was a desire for the Lord to move mightily in the hearts of the people.

The Bible says, *"The burden which Habakkuk the prophet did see."* It was a burden he did *"see"* not feel. His burden was for God to do what only God could do. *[handwritten: supernaturalism]* *[handwritten: Note: He did not want to "feel something" But He want to "see" God move]*

[handwritten: We need God to do something we can not do]

A Dark Hour of Human History

Habakkuk was living in a dark hour of human history. In the book of Jeremiah, we get insight into Habakkuk's day and what was going on in his land. Remember that Habakkuk and Jeremiah served the Lord under King Jehoiakim, just as Nebuchadnezzar, king of Babylon, was preparing his army to conquer Judah and take captive the people of God. In this same day in which Habakkuk served, God spoke to Jeremiah about the message he was to take to King Jehoiakim. Remember, the Jews are God's chosen people, the people that God had raised up from Abraham to be the people to whom and through whom He would make Himself known to the whole world. These are the people to whom God gave His Word and through whom God sent His Son, the Lord Jesus Christ, to pay our sin debt.

The Bible says in Jeremiah 36:1-7,

> *And it came to pass in the fourth year of Jehoiakim the son of Josiah king of Judah, that this word came unto Jeremiah from the LORD, saying, Take thee a roll of a book, and write therein all the words that I have spoken unto thee against Israel, and against Judah, and against all the nations, from the day I spake unto thee, from the days of Josiah, even unto this day. It may be that the house of Judah will hear all the evil which I purpose to do unto them; that they may return every man from his evil way; that I may forgive their iniquity and their sin. Then Jeremiah called Baruch the son of Neriah: and Baruch wrote from the mouth of Jeremiah all the words of the LORD, which he had spoken unto him, upon a roll of a book. And Jeremiah commanded Baruch, saying, I am shut up; I cannot go into the house of the LORD: therefore go thou, and read in the roll, which thou hast written from my mouth, the words of the LORD in the ears of the people in the LORD's house upon the fasting day: and also thou shalt read them in the ears of all Judah that come out of their cities. It may be they will present their supplication before the LORD, and will return every one from his evil way: for great is the*

anger and the fury that the LORD hath pronounced against this people.

God told Jeremiah to send this message to the king and to the people. If they heard the message of God and turned from their evil ways, the Lord would forgive their sin. God gave the people an opportunity to repent.

The Bible continues in Jeremiah 36:8-24,

> And Baruch the son of Neriah did according to all that Jeremiah the prophet commanded him, reading in the book the words of the LORD in the LORD's house. And it came to pass in the fifth year of Jehoiakim the son Josiah king of Judah, in the ninth month, that they proclaimed a fast before the LORD to all the people in Jerusalem, and to all the people that came from the cities of Judah unto Jerusalem. Then read Baruch in the book the words of Jeremiah in the house of the LORD, in the chamber of Gemariah the son of Shaphan the scribe, in the higher court, at the entry of the new gate of the LORD's house, in the ears of all the people. When Michaiah the son of Gemariah, the son of Shaphan, had heard out of the book all the words of the LORD, then he went down into the king's house, into the scribe's chamber: and, lo, all the princes sat there, even Elishama the scribe, and Delaiah the son of Shemaiah, and Elnathan the son of Achbor, and Gemariah the son of Shaphan, and Zedekiah the son of Hananiah, and all the princes. Then Michaiah declared unto them all the words that he had heard, when Baruch read the book in the ears of the people. Therefore all the princes sent Jehudi the son of Nethaniah, the son of Shelemiah, the son of Cushi, unto Baruch, saying, Take in thine hand the roll wherein thou hast read in the ears of the people, and come. So Baruch the son of Neriah took the roll in his hand, and came unto them.

And they said unto him, Sit down now, and read it in our ears. So Baruch read it in their ears. Now it came to pass, when they had heard all the words, they were afraid both one and other, and said unto Baruch, We will surely tell the king of all these words.

These scribes and princes heard the word of Jeremiah and they said they would tell the king *"all these words."*

And they asked Baruch, saying, Tell us now, How didst thou write all these words at his mouth? Then Baruch answered them, He pronounced all these words unto me with his mouth, and I wrote them with ink in the book. Then said the princes unto Baruch, Go, hide thee, thou and Jeremiah; and let no man know where ye be. And they went in to the king into the court, but they laid up the roll in the chamber of Elishama the scribe, and told all the words in the ears of the king. So the king sent Jehudi to fetch the roll: and he took it out of Elishama the scribe's chamber. And Jehudi read it in the ears of the king, and in the ears of all the princes which stood beside the king.

Now remember, he was reading this to the king of Judah; the king of the chosen people of God. He was reading the Word of God from the man of God.

Now the king sat in the winter house in the ninth month: and there was a fire on the hearth burning before him. And it came to pass, that when Jehudi had read three or four leaves, he cut it with the penknife, and cast it into the fire that was on the hearth, until all the roll was consumed in the fire that was on the hearth. Yet they were not afraid, nor rent their garments, neither the king, nor any of his servants that heard all these words.

LORD, SEND A REVIVAL

When the king heard the Word of God, he cut it with his knife and threw it into the fire. By his actions he declared, "We will not have God, and we will not have God's Word!" This is the dark hour in which Habakkuk lived. "We do not want God, and we do not want God's Word!" Read on in the passage and discover the most frightening thing, *"Yet they were not afraid."* There was no fear of God before their eyes.

No wonder the Bible says, *"The burden which Habakkuk the prophet did see."* He saw the darkness around him, and he was burdened for God to move upon the scene.

What Habakkuk feared would happen did happen. After the awful captivity took place, the 137th Psalm was written. The Bible says in Psalm 137:1, *"By the rivers of Babylon, there we sat down, yea, we wept, when we remembered Zion."* God's people thought of Zion. They thought of how their lives used to be.

Psalm 137:2-9 says,

> *We hanged our harps upon the willows in the midst thereof. For there they that carried us away captive required of us a song; and they that wasted us required of us mirth, saying, Sing us one of the songs of Zion. How shall we sing the LORD's song in a strange land? If I forget thee, O Jerusalem, let my right hand forget her cunning. If I do not remember thee, let my tongue cleave to the roof of my mouth; if I prefer not Jerusalem above my chief joy. Remember, O LORD, the children of Edom in the day of Jerusalem; who said, Rase it, rase it, even to the foundation thereof. O daughter of Babylon, who art to be destroyed; happy shall he be, that rewardeth thee as thou hast served us. Happy shall he be, that taketh and dasheth thy little ones against the stones.*

Evidently, the people had seen their little ones taken by the hands of their Babylonian captors and their heads bashed against the stones. Not

CHAPTER TWO

The Question All People Ask and No One Can Answer

T he name *Habakkuk* means "one who embraces." Habakkuk wrapped his arms around the Lord and prayed, asking God for an answer. This man's heart was stirred because of the condition of his nation. Although Habakkuk's prayer was given centuries ago, he asked the same questions and dealt with the same problems that we deal with today.

The Word of God says in Habakkuk 1:1-4,

> *The burden which Habakkuk the prophet did see. O LORD, how long shall I cry, and thou wilt not hear! even cry out unto thee of violence, and thou wilt not save! Why dost thou show me iniquity, and cause me to behold grievance? for spoiling and violence are before me: and there are that raise up strife and contention. Therefore the law is slacked, and judgment doth never go forth: for*

the wicked doth compass about the righteous; therefore wrong judgment proceedeth.

Notice the little word *"Why?"* in Habakkuk 1:3. This is the question that all men ask and no man can answer. Habakkuk was a troubled man; he had a burdened heart. He lived in a dark hour of the history of his nation. He was desperate. He cried out to God declaring that the Lord would not hear. Then he asked God, "Why? Why is this going on? If God is eternal and almighty, why does He allow this? Why?"

Remember that the nation of Judah was on the eve of captivity. The prophet, Habakkuk, a contemporary of Jeremiah, was preaching and praying on the eve of the destruction of Judah. At this particular point in history, Babylon had become the mightiest nation in all the world. The nation was led by King Nebuchadnezzar, a famous king not only in biblical literature, but also in world history.

The Babylonian empire had as its capital the city of Babylon. The perimeter of the city was over sixty miles. The walls of the city were as high as a football field is long. They were wide enough for chariots to race around the tops of the walls. Inside the city of Babylon was one of the wonders of the ancient world–the Hanging Gardens. Mighty King Nebuchadnezzar had them built for his queen. Because of his might, Nebuchadnezzar felt he could do as he pleased and answer to no one. His desire was to take the nation of Judah.

Inside Judah, the people had turned against God. The king of Judah, Jehoiakim, had defied God and God's Word. The prophet Jeremiah had preached to him and said, "God has sent a message, and if you'll receive God's message and turn from your sin, the Lord will hear your prayer and spare your land." When King Jehoiakim heard the message, he took the Word of God, cut it into pieces with a penknife, and threw it into the fire, saying, "I don't want your God and I don't want His Word!"

If you had asked Habakkuk at that moment how things were going in his nation, you would find his answer in Habakkuk 1:3-4 when he cries out to God and says, *"Spoiling and violence are before me: and there are that raise up strife and contention. Therefore the law is slacked, and judgment doth never go forth: for the wicked doth compass about the righteous; therefore wrong judgment proceedeth."* It seemed to Habakkuk that the wicked were winning. The Word of God says in Psalm 12:8, *"The wicked walk on every side, when the vilest men are exalted."* In Habakkuk's day vile men were exalted.

Do you wonder today about our land? It seems as though the wicked are winning the battle of influence for good and evil.

As long ago as May 7, 1990, the cover article of *Time Magazine* read, "Dirty Words: America's Foul-mouthed Pop Culture." The article was about the music performers and comedians of our day. In the article, Lisette, a thirteen-year-old seventh-grader from Mamaroneck, New York, says she loves heavy metal and does not understand what all the fuss is about. This thirteen year old made this comment about heavy metal bands,

> A lot of adults don't like them because when they're married and settled down, they don't think about having action or talking dirty. But teenagers do because of their sexual peak. If songs have curses in them, they're not going to bother kids. Everyone knows swear words by the third grade. My advice to parents is to let your kids grow up and do what they want to do.

As we think about the spiritual darkness in our beloved country, we are tempted to ask God, "Why? Why does God allow such things to take place?" All of us ask, "Why?" Many times during tragedy, people say, "I know I'm not supposed to ask, but I wonder why this is happening." There are times when it seems that our problems are insurmountable; we have no idea what to do, but we know there is a God in heaven and we wonder why God allows these things to take place. Perhaps something takes place that can never be corrected or changed. When this happens, we wonder why God allowed it.

Early in my ministry, a young man came to see me and showed me one little black mark on his thumbnail. He and his wife had been faithfully serving the Lord in the church. He said, "I've been to the doctor. I didn't know why this little mark was on my thumbnail." Then he said, "Pastor, they just told me that I have one of the rarest forms of cancer ever diagnosed. They say there is no hope for a cure and that within months, I'll be dead."

As he and his wife sat in my place of study that day, we cried together. They did not ask the question that day, but they had it on their hearts, "Why has God allowed this to happen to us?"

When I was a fourteen-year-old boy, my mother walked across the street, on Easter Sunday, to tell my brother and me that my father was dead. She found us playing in a field. When we heard that awful news, we wondered, "Why?"

If you have not asked, you will ask some day, "Why? If there is a God, and He is almighty, why does He allow certain things to happen? Why?"

This question was on the heart of the disciples as they traveled with the Lord Jesus one day. The Bible says in John 9:1-4,

> *And as Jesus passed by, he saw a man which was blind from his birth. And his disciples asked him, saying, Master, who did sin, this man, or his parents, that he was born blind? Jesus answered, Neither hath this man sinned, nor his parents: but that the works of God should be made manifest in him. I must work the works of him that sent me, while it is day: the night cometh, when no man can work.*

The disciples wanted to know why this man had been born blind. Why had God allowed this to take place? Was it because of his sin or the sin of his parents?

Notice what the Lord Jesus said in response to their question, *"Neither hath this man sinned, nor his parents: but that the works of God should be made manifest in him."*

Someone may ask, "Why has God allowed this terrible thing to take place in my home? Why doesn't God save my son? Why doesn't God bring my daughter back? Why has God allowed my husband to leave me? Why is all this going on?" This question *"Why?"* is a question that all people ask, but no one has the answer.

In God's Word we find principles that we need to get into our hearts that help us to deal with this question, *"Why?"*

WE ARE LOVED OF GOD

The first principle that we need to understand is that we are loved of God. We cannot understand anything else until we realize that God loves us. He tells us in Jeremiah 31:3, *"Yea, I have loved thee with an everlasting love."* There is nothing we can do to make God stop loving us. There is nothing we can do to make God love us more than He already loves us. It does not make any difference where we came from or what our parents did or did not do, God loves us.

The victory is in the Person of Jesus Christ as we trust Him.

You may have grown up in a very wicked home and had wicked parents, but God loves those parents as much as God loves you. One of the things that is incomprehensible to the human mind is that the vilest people in all the world are still loved of God. It is easy for us to love certain people. We have no problem at all showing affection and attention to those "easy-to-love" people. Our hearts are moved and stirred when we think about them. But God loves all people, even the vilest of sinners.

There has never been a time in my life when God did not love me. There has never been a time in my life when God did not see me and know what was going on in my life. He loves me no matter what I do, no matter what I become or do not become. God loves me.

The Bible says in John 3:16, *"For God so loved the world, that he gave his only begotten Son, that whosoever believeth in him should not perish, but have everlasting life."* Let us establish this fact before we deal with anything else—we are loved of God.

Remember that the Devil is an accuser of the brethren and he will accuse you. He will accuse God to you and you to God. He will feed your mind with all kinds of fallacies that do not agree with God's Word. The Devil is a liar. He will tell you that God does not love you and does not care about you; because, if He loved you, He would not have let certain things happen to you. This simply is not true. God loves you.

God's Thoughts Are Not Our Thoughts

The Bible says in Isaiah 55:8-11,

> *For my thoughts are not your thoughts, neither are your ways my ways, saith the LORD. For as the heavens are higher than the earth, so are my ways higher than your ways, and my thoughts than your thoughts. For as the rain cometh down, and the snow from heaven, and returneth not thither, but watereth the earth, and maketh it bring forth and bud, that it may give seed to the sower, and bread to the eater: so shall my word be that goeth forth out of my mouth: it shall not return unto me void, but it shall accomplish that which I please, and it shall prosper in the thing whereto I sent it.*

The Bible says that God's thoughts are not our thoughts. God does not think the way we think. We are bound by certain limitations in our thinking. We have points of reference that are a part of our makeup. One of our biggest problems is trying to squeeze God into some man-made image. We try to make God into our image and bring Him to our way of thinking, imagining that God works the same way we work. But if we are going to deal with this question, *"Why?"* we must learn that God loves us and that God does not think the way we think.

GOD'S WAYS ARE NOT OUR WAYS

The Bible says, *"For my thoughts are not your thoughts, neither are your ways my ways, saith the LORD."* God's ways are not our ways. We think the way to work is to match flesh against flesh and work our way through our problems and overcome them with human ingenuity. But God does not work that way. God is able to do anything He pleases in any way He pleases to do it, but His ways are not our ways. He is holy. His way is always right.

THE LORD IS NOT ON OUR TIMETABLE

The Bible says in II Peter 3:9-10,

The Lord is not slack concerning his promise, as some men count slackness; but is longsuffering to us-ward, not willing that any should perish, but that all should come to repentance. But the day of the Lord will come as a thief in the night; in the which the heavens shall pass away with a great noise, and the elements shall melt with fervent heat, the earth also and the works that are therein shall be burned up.

The Lord speaks in II Peter chapter three about His coming again. He is talking about the concluding of human history as we know it. Notice that He states in verse eight, *"But beloved, be not ignorant of this one thing, that one day is with the Lord as a thousand years, and a thousand years as one day."* The thing we must realize is that God does not work on the same timetable as we do. I want my problems solved now. We all want everything worked out now. But in all our dealing with the "Why?" of life, we must remember that God loves us; that He thinks a different way than we think; that He works a different way than the way we work, and that He has a different timetable than the timetable we have.

The Christian life is a faith life.

God is able to do things over a period of time that we never thought could be accomplished. Think about how we can laugh about some things today that we cried over years ago. We can smile about some things that we thought we could not live through when they were taking place. God's timetable is not our timetable.

THE ANSWER IS THE LORD JESUS CHRIST

The Bible says in II Corinthians 5:7-9, *"For we walk by faith, not by sight: we are confident, I say, and willing rather to be absent from the body, and to be present with the Lord. Wherefore we labour, that, whether present or absent, we may be accepted of him."*

Verse seven says, *"For we walk by faith, not by sight."* If we must have an answer for every question, we are actually saying to the Lord, "I want to live by sight. I cannot live unless God lets me know why. I must be able to see why." Demanding an answer is saying, "Lord I must have sight of this thing." The Bible says that we are to walk by faith and not by sight. What God wants us to find out is that our answer is the

Person of Jesus Christ and our dependence must be on Him. If everything we depend on does not turn out the way we hoped it would, we can still be victorious through the Person of Jesus Christ.

Try to explain why your children are born healthy and someone else, who has tried to live as good as you, has children who are not born healthy. Try to explain why someone who has been faithful all the days of his life to the Lord is told at age twenty that he is dying with cancer. We need to be willing to admit that we do not have all the answers. Many good people are trying to give answers who do not have answers. People wonder, "Why?" What we need to do through our "Why?" is trust the Lord, realizing that He will take care of us.

The Word of God says in I John 5:4, *"For whatsoever is born of God overcometh the world: and this is the victory that overcometh the world, even our faith."*

We learn many things as we travel through this book of Habakkuk, but I do not believe we will learn anything more important than the principle that we must stop trying to get an answer and start looking for the victory in the Lord. This is a book about trusting God. The victory is in the Person of Jesus Christ as we trust Him. *"And this is the victory that overcometh the world, even our faith"* (I John 5:4).

The Christian life is a faith life. All men, in their human nature say, "God, why?" And there is no answer. No one can adequately answer that question. May God help us to stop looking for the answer and start looking for the victory. The victory is in trusting Jesus Christ, realizing He knows best and He will always do right. Habakkuk did not understand why God did not move quickly to judge the nation of Judah. After the Lord revealed to him the news of the coming destruction by Babylon, he realized things were even worse than he imagined. He came to the place where the Lord Himself became the answer. Putting his faith in the Lord in his uncertain time was his answer. The Lord Jesus Christ not only *has* the answers to life's great questions; He *is* the answer! The message of the book of Habakkuk is the message of faith in God. He never changes.

"Behold ye among the heathen, and regard, and wonder marvellously: for I will work a work in your days, which ye will not believe, though it be told you."

Habakkuk 1:5

Remember, God Is at Work

In this book of Habakkuk, the prophet spoke to God and God spoke back to him. Habakkuk cried out to God, "Lord, why is this happening? How long is this going to continue?" It looked to him as if the wicked were winning. Then there was a moment of silence, and the silence was broken as God spoke to Habakkuk in chapter one, verses five through eleven, saying,

Behold ye among the heathen, and regard, and wonder marvellously: for I will work a work in your days, which ye will not believe, though it be told you. For, lo, I raise up the Chaldeans, that bitter and hasty nation, which shall march through the breadth of the land, to possess the dwelling places that are not their's. They are terrible and dreadful: their judgment and their dignity shall proceed of themselves. Their horses also are swifter than the leopards, and are more fierce than the evening wolves: and their horsemen shall spread themselves, and their horsemen shall come from far; they shall fly as the eagle that hasteth to eat. They shall come all for violence: their faces shall sup up as the east wind, and they shall gather the captivity as the sand. And they shall scoff at the kings, and the princes shall be a scorn unto them: they shall deride every stronghold; for they shall heap dust, and take it. Then shall his mind change, and he shall pass over, and offend, imputing this his power unto his god.

Did the Lord ever tell you anything you did not want to hear? Did you ever find anything in the Bible that you did not want to read? Did you ever discover anything about the Lord's work in the world that you wished you had not discovered, at least for that moment? We can be assured that when God spoke these words to Habakkuk, his heart was deeply troubled. It was one of those situations where he would have said, "I wish I'd never asked the question."

The nation of Judah was spiritually bankrupt. They had turned from God. Habakkuk was troubled about his own people and their sin. Then the Lord said to him, "I'm going to bring the heathen nation of Babylon down upon Judah and I'm going to use them to bring judgment upon my people."

To Habakkuk this must have looked like a bad situation that just got worse. In the midst of this perplexing problem, God declared to the prophet, *"I will work a work."* This is a promise God made to Habakkuk, a promise that God is always at work.

When we are faced with what seems to be an impossible situation, we need to remember that God is at work. It may be that God is working in the most unlikely place and in the most unlikely way, but He is at work. The Lord said in the fifth verse, *"Behold ye among the heathen, and regard, and wonder marvellously."* Can you imagine this? Habakkuk said, "Lord, it's Your people, these Jews, who have a need. How are You going to bring these people back to Yourself?"

The Lord answered, *"Behold ye among the heathen."*

Habakkuk thought, "What? You don't understand, Lord; I'm talking about Judah. I'm praying that You will work in Judah. I'm asking You to work in the lives of Your people."

But the Lord said, *"Behold ye among the heathen."* The Lord declared to Habakkuk that He was going to begin His work in the most unlikely place to accomplish what needed to be accomplished in the lives of His people.

Remember that His ways are not our ways and His thoughts are not our thoughts; nevertheless, God is at work!

There is a precious promise in the Bible that we need to remember. God's Word says in Philippians 1:6, *"Being confident of this very thing, that he which hath begun a good work in you will perform it until the day of Jesus Christ."*

> *When we are faced with what seems to be an impossible situation, we need to remember that God is at work.*

Paul declared his confidence in the fact that God will finish what He has started. This brings great comfort to my heart.

If you get in the middle of someone's troubles, you may wonder how anything good could ever come out of that seemingly impossible situation. Remember, God is at work and He is not finished yet.

THE CARELESSNESS OF GOD'S PEOPLE

The Lord said to the prophet in Habakkuk 1:5, *"Behold ye among the heathen, and regard, and wonder marvellously: for I will work a work in your days, which ye will not believe, though it be told you."*

The Lord said, "I'm going to share it with you, but when I share it with you, you won't believe it."

Our great need is for people who say that they are Christians to live as Christians. If we are saved, we need to live like saved people–loving, compassionate, tender, forgiving, kind–like the Lord Jesus. What we need in our churches is for people to simply behave as Christians. What we need in business places, if there is a Christian there, is for that Christian to conduct his life like a Christian. He should be truthful, honest, decent, God-fearing; he should simply be a Christian. Instead, God's people have developed a carelessness that is alarming.

> *Our great need is for people who say that they are Christians to live as Christians. What we need in our churches is for people to simply behave as Christians.*

Hundreds of years after God gave this message to Habakkuk, the apostle Paul used a verse from Habakkuk in one of his messages. In the thirteenth chapter of the book of Acts, Paul was declaring to the people what God was going to do and how God would bring to pass certain things. In the middle of his message, Paul said in Acts 13:40-41, *"Beware therefore, lest that come upon you, which is spoken of in the prophets; behold, ye despisers, and wonder, and perish: for I work a work in your days, a work which ye shall in no wise believe, though a man declare it unto you."*

Paul said, "I want you to be careful, because you are going to live so carelessly in your Christian lives that you will forget that God can do all things." He is the God of the impossible. God can hear and answer prayer. God can change lives. God can work miracles. God can save to the uttermost. God can take people who do not care anything about His work or His church and turn their lives around. But, if we are not careful, we will begin to doubt God and what God can do.

There is a carelessness about our faith in God. It is really a refusal to believe that God is able to do all things.

God declared to the prophet Habakkuk the same thing Paul declared in this message in Acts chapter thirteen—we must guard against a spirit of unbelief!

THE CRUELTY OF THOSE WHO DO NOT KNOW THE LORD

Just how cruel can people be? Beginning in Habakkuk 1:6, God gives a description of the Babylonians coming down upon Judah. Most people have the idea that someday God is going to bring judgment in one final sweeping blow. Remember that judgment is also progressive. For example, you may walk out into your yard after a storm and notice that a tree has fallen. If you look carefully, you may notice that the tree had been decaying for years, slowly but surely rotting on the inside, then, the final blow came when a gust of wind blew it over.

If you are afraid that one of these days our nation is going to be judged, remember that we are also being judged now. The judgment of God is sure. We reap what we sow, and we suffer because of months and years of neglect. There are specific judgments spoken of in God's Word that are not being addressed in this context. What we are discussing is the fact that we are being judged on a daily basis for our neglect of the things of God.

> *God declared to the prophet Habakkuk the same thing Paul declared in this message in Acts chapter thirteen—we must guard against a spirit of unbelief!*

God said to Habakkuk, *"For, lo, I raise up the Chaldeans, that bitter and hasty nation, which shall march through the breadth of the land, to possess the dwelling places that are not their's."* It is not their land, but they are going to take it. They are terrible and dreadful. They have no mercy.

God's Word says in Habakkuk 1:7-11,

> *They are terrible and dreadful: their judgment and their dignity shall proceed of themselves. Their horses also are swifter than the leopards, and are more fierce than the evening wolves: and their horsemen shall spread themselves, and their horsemen shall come from far; they shall fly as the eagle that hasteth to eat. They shall come all for violence: their faces shall sup up as the east wind, and they shall gather the captivity as the sand. And they shall scoff at the kings, and the princes shall be a scorn unto them: they shall deride every stronghold; for they shall heap dust, and take it. Then shall his mind change, and he shall pass over, and offend, imputing this his power unto his god.*

The cruelest thing of all is that the Babylonians attributed their greatness to their gods. They said that their gods were greater than the God of Judah. Think how our unbelief dishonors the true and living God.

Why are people so cruel? Why is there such cruelty in the world? There is great cruelty in the world because people have turned their hearts from the true God.

A British historian named Thomas McCauley, a man who died just before the Civil War began, wrote an interesting statement about America. He lived and died much more than a century ago. This historian said of America,

> Your republic, America, will be fearfully plundered and laid waste by barbarians in the twentieth century as the Roman Empire was in the fifth, with this difference: that the Huns and Vandals who ravaged the Roman Empire came from without, and your Huns and Vandals

will have been engendered within your own country. By your own institutions you will be destroyed.

Judah was falling from within because of her sin. The nation was imploding. Unbelief was at the heart of her judgment. The cruel Babylonians were only the instrument of God's judgment. As we think about the recent tragedies in America, we have reason to ask, "Are these instruments of God's judgment?"

THE COMPASSION OF OUR LORD

We must never forget that our God is a God of compassion. One of the things I believe yet do not understand is that no man can go so low that God does not continue to love him and desire to save him. The Bible says, *"He is not willing that any should perish."* No boy can be such a rebel; no daughter such a disappointment; no daddy such a vile human being; no mother such a godless woman; no human being can get so far from the Lord that God does not still love him and desire to save him.

No human being can get so far from the Lord that God does not still love him and desire to save him.

Have you ever wondered if God knew your problems? Has there ever been a time when you lay awake at night because you were so overcome by your troubles? You may have said, "Lord, don't You know where I am? Don't You know what's going on? Don't You care what is happening to me?" There is a God in heaven who wants to send us a message. The message is, "Remember, I'm working. I'm working. Though you don't see it right now, I will work a work. I'm working."

Perhaps the most beautiful story of the Bible is in the fifteenth chapter of the Gospel according to Luke. One day a boy came to his father and said,

"I'm leaving. Give me what's coming to me. I'm getting out of this house." The Bible says he, *"took his journey into a far country, and there wasted his substance with riotous living."* His father loved him dearly. He could only imagine what was going on in the life of his son, but he loved him. Of course, Christ is speaking of the love of our heavenly Father in this story. The hard thing for me to understand is how that father could go to bed at night; how he could rest at night, wondering where his boy was; how he and his wife did not argue and fuss about it; how he could get up and go to work and function in some normal fashion. It is a marvel to me. But do you know why he could do it? Because he did not have his faith and confidence in that boy. He loved him and looked for him every day, but he had his faith and confidence in the fact that God loved his son and that God was going to work in the heart of his son. The boy came to himself and came home to his father.

> *We need to anchor our faith again in the compassion of our God and the fact that the Lord is at work.*

Most of us have placed our confidence in wrong things. We need to anchor our faith again in the compassion of our God and the fact that the Lord is at work. He will accomplish a work that only He can accomplish in our lives and in the lives of those we love. Remember God said, *"I will work a work."*

"Art thou not from everlasting, O
LORD my God, mine Holy One?
we shall not die. O LORD, thou
hast ordained them for judgment;
and, O mighty God, thou hast
established them for correction."

Habakkuk 1:12

The God I Know

Y ears ago someone placed in my hands a book entitled *Your God Is Too Small*. I do not recommend the book, but I do recommend that we give thought to the title, *Your God Is Too Small*. Most of us say that we know God, but there are many times in our lives when we act as if our Lord is incapable of dealing with the complex problems and needs of this troubled world.

Habakkuk cried unto the Lord in Habakkuk 1:12-17,

Art thou not from everlasting, O LORD my God, mine Holy One? we shall not die. O LORD, thou hast ordained them for judgment; and, O mighty God, thou hast established them for correction. Thou are of purer eyes than to behold evil, and canst not look on iniquity: wherefore lookest thou upon them that deal treacherously, and holdest thy tongue when the wicked devoureth the man that is more righteous than he? And makest men as the fishes of the sea, as the creeping things, that have no ruler over them? They take up all of them with the angle, they catch them in their net, and gather them in their drag: therefore they rejoice and are glad. Therefore they sacrifice unto their net, and burn incense unto their drag; because by them their portion is fat, and their meat plenteous. Shall they therefore empty their net, and not spare continually to slay the nations?

Notice as Habakkuk answered the Lord he used the expression, *"O LORD my God."*

The prophet Habakkuk stood on the eve of the captivity of Judah. The burden of his heart brought him to God. As he spoke to the Lord about the sins of his own people, he said, "Lord, I don't understand why Your people can live as they live and You don't deal with them." Do you ever wonder why God does not break through the heavens and bring judgment suddenly upon someone? As Habakkuk looked at God's people, he said, "Lord, I don't understand how they can live in sin, how they can have a king who says, 'I want no Bible, I want no God telling me what to do.' I don't understand how we can have a nation like that and You don't judge it." Then God said to him, "Habakkuk, I'm going to judge Judah. The Babylonians are moving down from the north to invade the land." Then the Lord began to describe the Babylonians and what they were going to do to Judah. Suddenly Habakkuk's heart was filled with terror and he cried out to God, "Lord, I know that we are in sin, but they are worse. We know the true God. The Babylonians don't know the true God. How can they come down upon us?"

Habakkuk was troubled. He did not know what to do or where to turn. In answer to God, he recounted to the Lord the things that he knew to be true about God. He spoke of the God that he knew. What do you know to be true about God?

There are certain things that characterize our age. We are living in a time when there is no fear of God before the eyes of people. We are living in an age of confusion. Parents are confused about what to do with their children. Husbands and wives are confused about what to do in their marital relationships. The home is not a place of bliss and peace; it is a place of trouble. Churches are confused. Pastors are confused. The entire world seems to be moving into a state of confusion, and the Bible says that the Lord is not the author of confusion. So this confusion has been brought on by the prince and power of the air, the god of this world, the Devil. In our day, so similar to the day in which Habakkuk lived, we need to look again at the Word of God and to the God we know. Our God remains the same–He never changes. He promised in Malachi 3:6, *"For I am the LORD, I change not."*

Notice the expression Habakkuk uses, *"O LORD my God."* He uses the personal pronoun *"my."* Just as I know the Lord as my personal Savior, Habakkuk knew the Lord as his personal Savior. He was not some distant god millions of miles away that could not be reached, but rather a personal God that he knew. Habakkuk put his faith in Him; he could reach Him in the crisis hour. He had a personal relationship with God.

Do you know the Lord? I am not talking about how many things you can tell me *about* God, but do you *know* God? Was there a glad hour in your life when someone pointed you to Jesus Christ and you asked God to forgive your sin and by faith you received Jesus Christ as your personal Savior? Do you know that you have been born again?

Just as Habakkuk lived in a time of crisis, we are living in a time of crisis. Look to the Lord Jesus Christ. Just as Habakkuk did, we need to review the things we know to be true about our God.

GOD IS ETERNAL

In Habakkuk 1:12 the Bible says, *"Art thou not from everlasting, O LORD my God, mine Holy One?"* The God we know is eternal. He had no beginning, and He has no ending. He is eternally existent. The Bible says in Genesis 1:1, *"In the beginning God created."* God's Word does not say, "In the beginning God" but *"In the beginning God created."* God had no beginning. He is eternal. He is the same yesterday, today, and forever. He has no ending.

When men come to know the Lord, they come to know the Lord who is eternal. In every generation of human history, men have been able by faith to know the true and living God who is eternal. This means, what God was able to do in generations long ago, He is able to do today. He is the God of this present hour because He is eternal. Habakkuk anchored his soul in this fact. He said, "I don't understand why God has not dealt with Judah; I don't understand why He is bringing Babylon down to judge us, but I know God and I know that God is eternal." This is what we need to know.

In Psalm 90:1-2 the Bible says, *"LORD, thou hast been our dwelling place in all generations. Before the mountains were brought forth, or ever thou hadst formed the earth and the world, even from everlasting to everlasting, thou art God."* God is eternal.

GOD IS SELF-EXISTENT

The expression, *"O LORD my God,"* means the God who is self-sustaining and self-existent. He depends on nothing to exist. He is eternally-existent; He is self-existent. We are dependent. We are dependent upon other people and things. As a matter of fact, the only way we got into this world was through the relationship of a man and woman we call Mom and Dad. Our beginning started with dependence. We are dependent upon the air we breathe. As our bodily functions are carried on, we are declaring our dependence. There is not a man or woman, though he may raise his voice against God and declare that he needs no one, who is not dependent. This is not so with God. God is self-existent. Without everything and without everyone, God still exists.

In Habakkuk's crisis hour when the treacherous Babylonians were about to sweep down over the nation of Judah and carry the young of the land away to captivity, this man of God was glad to know that he knew the Lord, personally, who was self-existent. No matter what happens in the world, though nations rise and nations fall, nothing is going to change the nature of God. He is eternal and self-existent.

GOD IS HOLY

Habakkuk said in verse twelve, *"Art thou not from everlasting, O LORD my God, mine Holy One?"* The God I know is holy.

We may say that God will not make a wrong decision, but the truth is God *cannot* make a wrong decision. All of this is grounded in the holiness of God; He is pure, perfect, and holy.

I do not know how strong your human relationships are. I do not know how strong your family is. But I know we all go through hours of testing and trial. In the awful hours, in the dark hours when the sun of life and happiness in human relationships refuses to shine, I hope you have learned that God remains the same. There will come a time in the life of every child of God when it seems that all he has left is the Lord Jesus. When that time comes, know in your heart that God is holy and He will do right.

No matter what happens in the world, though nations rise and nations fall, nothing is going to change the nature of God.

Habakkuk said, "Lord, I can't understand what is going on, but I know the God who is eternal, self-existent, and holy."

In I Peter 1:15-16 the Bible says, *"But as he which hath called you is holy, so be ye holy in all manner of conversation; because it is written, Be ye holy; for I am holy."*

GOD IS FAITHFUL

There is a tremendous truth tucked away and may not be found with only a casual reading, but we must uncover it. In verse twelve of chapter one, Habakkuk said to the Lord, *"Art thou not from everlasting,* [eternal] *O LORD my God,* [self-existent] *mine Holy One?* [holy] *we shall not die."* What does Habakkuk mean by the expression, *"We shall not die"*? Habakkuk was a Jew. He knew that God had raised up the nation of Israel from the bosom of Abraham and that He had called Abraham from Ur of the Chaldees, the land from which the Babylonians were coming to attack Judah. He knew God had promised to Abraham that Abraham's seed would be as the stars of the heaven and the sands of the sea. Through Abraham all the nations of the earth would be blessed. Habakkuk knew that God had made that promise. That Abrahamic covenant had been enlarged upon by the covenant God made with David. The Lord promised through David that the throne of the Son of David would be established forever and that His people could not and would not be removed from the earth. God says, "I'm going to judge Israel; I'll scatter them; I'll bring Babylon down; I'll carry them into captivity; Jerusalem will lay waste; judgment is going to fall upon the place!"

There will come a time in the life of every child of God when it seems that all he has left is the Lord Jesus.

It looked as if everything concerning God's chosen people would be swept from the face of the earth. And Habakkuk said, "Lord, I remember a promise made to Israel and I know we shall not be utterly destroyed. We shall not die. The Jews will remain in the earth." God is faithful to His Word.

We also realize that the God we know is faithful. This means that I can lose my health; I can lose friends; I can lose loved ones; I can lose everything this world has, but the most devastating thing that could happen to me is that I would die and go to heaven. This is God's promise to the Christian. He will never leave us and He will never forsake us. God is faithful.

We know that our God is faithful no matter what trouble we face.

At this moment you may be experiencing very difficult times. We are not going to get out of this world without trouble because *"Man that is born of a woman is of few days, and full of trouble"* (Job 14:1). But we know that our God is faithful no matter what trouble we face. Habakkuk said, "We shall not die. The Jew will not completely vanish from the earth. This is according to the promise of God, and God is faithful to His Word."

The God I know is faithful. In the crisis hours of our lives, let us remember that He is faithful. We can count on God to keep His Word.

GOD IS ALMIGHTY

Let us remember also that God is almighty. The Bible says in Habakkuk 1:12, *"O mighty God, thou hast established them for correction."* The God I know is almighty. If we live by faith and through prayer and fasting seek God's face for things we need, we will not be surprised when God moves upon the scene and does what only He can do.

Here Habakkuk stood on the eve of the captivity of his nation. What would you think if someone said, "You are going to be overtaken by a strange land. You can muster all the armies you can gather together, but they will not save you. You will fall as a nation. Everything you ever dreaded that could go wrong is going to happen to you"? This is what Habakkuk faced. What should he do? He said, "Though I don't have a country and though I don't have a homeland, I still have God. He is eternal. He's self-existent. He's holy. He's faithful. He's almighty."

One day every voice as one mighty thundering chorus will declare, "The Lord God omnipotent reigneth."

The Bible says in Revelation 19:6, *"And I heard as it were the voice of a great multitude, and as the voice of many waters, and as the voice of mighty thunderings, saying, Alleluia: for the Lord God omnipotent reigneth."* One day every voice as one mighty thundering chorus will declare, *"The Lord God omnipotent reigneth."* We must remember that our God is still in control.

The God I know loves us and He sent His Son to earth to die for us. When Jesus Christ hung upon the cross of Calvary, He bled and died for our sins. He is the way to bring God and man together. He tasted death for every man and paid our sin debt on the cross of Calvary. He was buried and rose from the dead. This God I know, you can come to know also, when you are willing to ask Him to forgive your sin and by faith trust His Son for your salvation.

When we come to know Jesus Christ, we find that He is a wonderful Savior. He is faithful and He is able to do all things. He is in control. In a world of doubt and confusion, we must keep our eyes on Him and rest by faith in the God we know.

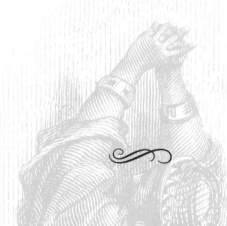

*"Behold, his soul which is lifted
up is not upright in him: but the
just shall live by his faith."*

Habakkuk 2:4

CHAPTER FIVE

Living by Faith

I n our complex world there is nothing as important as learning how to listen to the Lord. God loves us and desires to guide our lives.

The Bible says in Habakkuk 2:1-4,

I will stand upon my watch, and set me upon the tower, and will watch to see what he will say unto me, and what I shall answer when I am reproved. And the LORD answered me, and said, Write the vision, and make it plain upon tables, that he may run that readeth it. For the vision is yet for an appointed time, but at the end it shall speak, and not lie: though it tarry, wait for it; because it will surely come, it will not tarry. Behold, his soul which is lifted up is not upright in him: but the just shall live by his faith.

The prophet said in verse one of chapter two that he was going to stand before God and wait for God to reprove him–to tell him where he was wrong. God is holy; He is perfect. We are unholy; we are imperfect. Our holy God desires to tell unholy people what they are to do. Habakkuk did the right thing by listening for the Lord to reprove him.

Notice that the Bible says in Habakkuk 2:2, *"And the Lord answered me."* We have a God who answers men. When we are willing to listen and ready to hear Him, God will answer us. The Bible says in Hebrews 11:6, *"For he that cometh to God must believe that he is, and that he is a rewarder of them that diligently seek him."*

Habakkuk understood that Judah had forsaken the Lord, and the Lord answered Habakkuk by letting him know that the Babylonians were going to sweep down upon Judah and carry the people captive to Babylon. Habakkuk replied to the Lord by declaring that the Babylonians were more wicked than his people. How could God do such a thing?

Waiting on God is the time God uses to prepare our hearts to be able to hear His answer.

It is extremely difficult to wait on God because this waiting must be done by faith. We sometimes believe that the time we spend waiting on God is wasted, but it is not wasted. It is the time God uses to prepare our hearts to be able to hear His answer. Most of us think we are so busy that we cannot take the time to listen to the voice of God. The God who made heaven and earth, God Eternal, spoke to Habakkuk and also desires to speak with us.

God declared in Habakkuk 2:4, *"Behold, his soul which is lifted up is not upright in him: but the just shall live by his faith."*

In all of the Bible, there is no greater statement made to the Christian than this statement in Habakkuk 2:4. This verse tells us what works in life when nothing else appears to be working.

Everything in the book of Habakkuk either leads to or flows from this verse. The Christian life is built around this verse. It has provided victory for many men and women who have given their lives for Jesus Christ. What is so important about it? It sounds so simple, yet it is life changing. The Bible says in Habakkuk 2:4, *"Behold, his soul which is lifted up is not upright in him: but the just shall live by his faith."*

God divides all the world in this verse. The phrase *"Behold, his soul which is lifted up is not upright in him..."* speaks of those who do not know God, and the phrase *"...but the just shall live by his faith"* speaks of the saved. The phrase *"Behold, his soul which is lifted up is not upright in him..."* speaks of the unrighteous, and the phrase *"...but the just shall live by his faith"* speaks of those who have placed their faith in the Lord Jesus Christ. The Bible says, *"There is none righteous, no, not one"* (Romans 3:10), but we are declared righteous when we trust Jesus Christ and His righteousness for our salvation. We are made righteous by the imputing of Christ's righteousness on our account (Romans 4:23-5:2). We are saved by the grace of God through faith, and the Lord instructs us to live by faith.

Habakkuk 2:4 is the battleground. In this verse we see the world versus the Word. In it we see the world without God versus the Word of God. Notice the last part of the verse where God says, *"But the just shall live by his faith."* Let us consider the question, "How Shall We Live?" God declares that we are to live by faith.

The Babylonians and all those who live like the Babylonians live on the first part of this verse, *"Behold, his soul which is lifted up is not upright in him..."* This is the way of the world. All those who know the Lord and live for the Lord are in the second part of this verse, *"...but the just shall live by his faith."*

The remainder of the second chapter of Habakkuk deals with the Babylonians and their worldly lifestyle. The third chapter of this book deals with the saved and shows us how they are to live. The entire Bible deals with those who live for the world and those who live for the Lord. All people are divided by those who live for the world and those who live by the Word of God. All of us are living one way or the other.

In all of the Bible, there is no greater statement made to the Christian than this statement in Habakkuk 2:4. This verse tells us what works in life when nothing else appears to be working.

After my mother and father were divorced, my father got permission from my mother to take me on a trip alone with him. He had been to the doctor, and the doctor had told him that he was not going to live much longer. He died within two years of the day he came to see me. We enjoyed a trip to the mountains that day, but his aim was more than a pleasure trip. We drove into the mountains to a high place near the top of one of the mountains. Dad was not feeling well. He pulled the car to the side of the road, turned off the engine, looked at me, and said, "I brought you all this way to try to make up for something. I've lived my whole life, and I've thrown it away. I've been to the doctor, and the doctor says that I'm going to die. I can't live any longer than two more years, and I feel as if I've failed you. I have brought you all this way to get you alone and say one thing. I want to ask you not to make the same mistakes with your life that I have made with mine."

My dad was crying. He did not know what his words would mean. He hoped that they would have an impact. They did! I have never forgotten what he said to me. He wanted me to know that he had lived for the world and ignored God. He had made a terrible mistake and did not want me to make the same mistake with my life. I was faced with a choice.

It is the same choice all of us face. The choice is simple, shall we live only for this world or shall we live according to the Word of God?

THE OBJECT OF OUR FAITH

The Bible says, *"But the just shall live by his faith."* The most important thing about faith is not having faith, but rather the object of our faith. Where is your faith placed? If you get into an automobile, you may have faith that the automobile will run and that the tires will not explode on the highway while traveling at a high speed. If you board an airplane, you have faith that the pilot can fly the plane and that all things have been checked mechanically. For the Christian, whether in the air or on the ground, we are always in God's hands. There is nothing more important about faith than the object of our faith. The object of our faith must be the Person of Jesus Christ.

Habakkuk 2:4 is the battleground. In this verse we see the world versus the Word.

Habakkuk 2:4 is quoted in Romans 1:17, Galatians 3:11, and Hebrews 10:38. The Lord wants us to trust Him. The Bible says concerning faith in Hebrews 12:1-2,

> *Wherefore seeing we also are compassed about with so great a cloud of witnesses, let us lay aside every weight, and the sin which doth so easily beset us, and let us run with patience the race that is set before us, looking unto Jesus the author and finisher of our faith; who for the joy that was set before him endured the cross, despising the shame, and is set down at the right hand of the throne of God.*

The Bible says that Christ is the author and finisher of our faith. In other words, we start with Him and we finish the faith life with Him. We are to walk by faith. I believe in Someone I have never seen. I am giving my whole life to Someone I have never seen with my human eyes. This is faith; this is not a leap in the dark; it is not unfounded. We must either trust the Lord or trust ourselves. The Lord Jesus Christ is God. He is co-equal, co-existent, eternally existent with God the Father and God the Holy Spirit. The Lord Jesus became a man, yet without sin. He did not cease to be God when He became a man. He was robed in flesh so He could die for my sins. He went to the cross after living a sinless life and paid my sin debt with His own blood. He was buried, He rose from the dead, He ascended to heaven, and He ever liveth to make intercession for me. He is alive!

The object of our faith must be Jesus Christ. I came to Him and gave my life to Him. I started with Him, and some day I shall finish the faith life with Him. He is the first and the last. There is nothing more important than the object of our faith, and our faith is in Jesus Christ. The Lord remains the same—yesterday, today, and forever.

I heard someone speak on Habakkuk 2:4 many years ago when I was going through a great crisis. At the time I thought it was going to be the hardest thing with which I would ever have to deal. God used this verse of Scripture as I sat in the audience and listened. The speaker asked this question: "What if what you hoped would go right goes wrong? What if what you are counting on never comes true? How then are you going to live? The only answer is that you can still live by faith trusting Jesus Christ even when things around you are not working out right."

How could Noah live when the entire world had turned against God? By faith. How could Abraham live in a strange land when everyone else turned to heathenism? By faith. How could Daniel, Shadrach, Meshach and Abednego go into Babylon and stay true to God? By faith. How did they live in victory? The object of their faith was none other than the Lord Jesus. *"The just shall live by his faith."* Our Lord has designed the

Christian life so that we are able to be victorious in Him no matter what is taking place around us.

THE OPPOSITE OF FAITH

What is the opposite of faith? We may understand the subject of faith better by seeing what faith is not. Most of us would quickly say, "If faith is believing and trusting the Lord, then the opposite of faith is unbelief." This is not the answer according to Habakkuk 2:4. The opposite of faith is pride.

The Bible says in verse four, *"Behold, his soul which is lifted up..."* This means pride. When we do not believe the Lord, it is because of pride. Pride says, "I can make it. I can handle this. I can work this out. I can get myself out of this trouble. I can unravel this confusion. I can come out on top of this. I can work my way up." All refusal to trust the Lord is caused by pride. Faith is described in Hebrews 11:1 as *"the substance of things hoped for, the evidence of things not seen."* Faith is defined in Hebrews 12:2 as *"looking unto Jesus."* We are either *"looking unto Jesus,"* or in pride we are looking unto self.

God said of the Babylonians, who were going to be used to come down and judge Judah, "They don't believe in Me because of pride." The opposite of faith is pride; these Babylonians were puffed up with pride.

> *Faith is described in Hebrews 11:1 as "the substance of things hoped for, the evidence of things not seen." Faith is defined in Hebrews 12:2 as "looking unto Jesus."*

The Bible says, *"Behold, his soul which is lifted up is not upright."* Not only is he puffed up, but he is also deceitful. The words *"not upright"* mean deceitful. Deceitfulness always follows pride. If you are a proud person and will not humble yourself before the Lord, you are full of deceit. You think you must connive, scheme, plan and outwit everyone just to prove you know more than everyone else knows. You attempt to manipulate your way through life and make the best deal out of everything. The faith life is not lived that way. The object of faith must be Jesus Christ, and the opposite of faith is pride.

THE OUTCOME OF FAITH

The Bible says, *"Behold, his soul which is lifted up is not upright in him: but the just shall live by his faith."* This is a powerful expression. The Bible says in Ephesians 2:1, *"And you hath he quickened, who were dead in trespasses and sins."* The Bible also says in I John 5:4, *"For whatsoever is born of God overcometh the world: and this is the victory that overcometh the world, even our faith."* The outcome of faith is the victorious life.

I do not like to see anyone fail. I do not like to see people have trouble, but proud people are headed for destruction.

The outcome of faith is the victorious life.

One of the media giants made a speech not long ago denying all his religious upbringing. He denied anything he had ever believed about the Bible. Sooner or later that man is going to learn that all people who are filled with pride will fail. I do not want it to happen to him, but it is written into the law of God that it will happen. The outcome of faith is victory; the outcome of pride is defeat and destruction.

This battle is between following the world or following the Word of God. The Bible says in I John 2:15-17,

Love not the world, neither the things that are in the world. If any man love the world, the love of the Father is not in him. For all that is in the world, the lust of the flesh, and the lust of the eyes, and the pride of life, is not of the Father, but is of the world. And the world passeth away, and the lust thereof: but he that doeth the will of God abideth for ever.

You may be having such a hard time that you wonder how you are going to live. How shall we live? *"The just shall live by his faith."* I wish many things were different, but I still have the Lord Jesus Christ. He is real and He will see me through this life in victory and bring me into His glorious presence.

"Shall not all these take up a parable against him, and a taunting proverb against him, and say, Woe to him that increaseth that which is not his! how long? and to him that ladeth himself with thick clay!"

Habakkuk 2:6

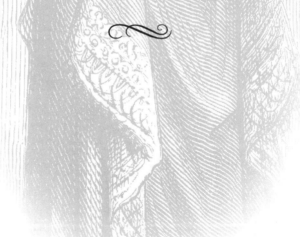

CHAPTER SIX

That's Not Yours

I n this journey we refer to as life, the greatest lesson we learn as Christians is that our Lord is trustworthy. We call this short book of Habakkuk one of the minor prophets, but it contains the major message of the Bible. This message is that God's people are to live by faith and the Lord will provide for us what we need as we trust Him. As we trust Him, He will take care of us.

Will He take care of us when things are not going the way we had planned for them to go and are not turning out the way we had planned for them to turn out?

This is exactly the situation in which Habakkuk the prophet of God found himself. He lived in the nation of Judah in an age when so many people, from the king all the way down to the lowliest citizens, had rejected the Lord. They refused to listen to God's Word or heed His warnings.

The prophet went to the Lord in prayer and God answered, *"Woe to him that increaseth that which is not his! how long? and to him that ladeth himself with thick clay!"* The Lord informed Habakkuk that He was going to bring the Babylonians down upon them and the Babylonian empire, the strongest in the world at that moment, would sweep down upon Judah and destroy the land, carrying the people of Judah captive to the land of Babylon.

When Habakkuk heard this, his heart was so stirred that he said, "Lord, how can You use such a wicked people to judge us? We are bad, but not as bad as they are." God explained to Habakkuk in Habakkuk 2:4-8,

> *Behold, his soul which is lifted up is not upright in him: but the just shall live by his faith. Yea also, because he transgresseth by wine, he is a proud man, neither keepeth at home, who enlargeth his desire as hell, and is as death, and cannot be satisfied, but gathereth unto him all nations, and heapeth unto him all people: shall not all these take up a parable against him, and a taunting proverb against him, and say, Woe to him that increaseth that which is not his! how long? and to him that ladeth himself with thick clay! Shall they not rise up suddenly that shall bite thee, and awake that shall vex thee, and thou shalt be for booties unto them? Because thou hast spoiled many nations, all the remnant of the people shall spoil thee; because of men's blood, and for the violence of the land, of the city, and of all that dwell therein.*

Please note what the Lord said in Habakkuk 2:6 when speaking of the nation of Babylon, *"Woe to him that increaseth that which is not his!"* Note especially the expression, *"which is not his."*

There are five times in the second chapter of Habakkuk that God says, *"Woe."* This word means "calamity and destruction." In the fourth verse of Habakkuk chapter two, God spoke about people living by faith. If we live by faith, we are trusting God. He sees all things from beginning to end. The God who sees all things will take care of us.

My confidence must not be in people and things; my confidence must be in God. The just, those who have been made righteous by faith in the Lord Jesus Christ, must live by faith. All the unsaved are in the other part of the fourth verse of chapter two, *"His soul which is lifted up is not upright in him."*

God pronounces these calamities or judgments upon the nation of Babylon. He says, "They are going to come!" He says, *"Woe to him that increaseth that which is not his!"* In the ninth verse He says, *"Woe to him that coveteth an evil coveteousness."* In the twelfth verse He says, *"Woe to him that buildeth a town with blood."* In the fifteenth verse He says, *"Woe unto him that giveth his neighbour drink."* In the nineteenth verse He says, *"Woe unto him that saith to the wood, Awake; to the dumb stone, Arise."*

God says there is certain judgment and calamity coming upon the nation of Babylon. This is certain. How many times have we brought wrinkles to our brow and fretting to our lives by wondering when God was going to take care of some problem? Leave it in God's hands! He will take care of the problems. We must remember that God says there are certain things that are not ours.

> *It is not what we have that matters; it is how we got what we have that matters.*

It is not what we have that matters; it is how we got what we have that matters. We are going to reap everything we have sown. The famous Nebuchadnezzar, who reigned on the throne of Babylon as king for sixty-three years, had gained his fame and prosperity in an evil way. This mighty king of Babylon, who thought he was the greatest of all that ever lived, was brought down to be like an animal grazing on the grass in the field. This mightiest of nations would fall. As we study the book of Habakkuk, let us look at each of these woes, these calamities and destructions that God pronounces.

The first one we consider is the one that involves stealing and robbing–taking that which is not yours.

In Exodus 20 we find the Ten Commandments. Verse fifteen says, *"Thou shalt not steal."* This is number eight of God's Ten Commandments. A man does not need to steal. If Jesus Christ is who He says He is, and He is, a man does not need to steal because the Lord said if we would seek Him first, He would provide for us all we need. This is what God's Word says in Matthew 6:33, *"But seek ye first the kingdom of God, and his righteousness; and all these things shall be added unto you."*

The nation of Babylon was running over everyone else, taking everything they wanted. God said, "They have built a kingdom on thievery and I am going to judge them for this."

We need to be careful about admiring people who have gotten gain the wrong way. They have God's judgment on their lives. They will fall some day. The Devil has a way of making wrong look right and right look wrong. You may think you are successful, but if you have followed the Devil's way in getting gain, God says you have failed.

You may think you have the victory, that you rule and reign and do as you please, but if you have taken the Devil's way of getting the victory, God says you are defeated.

The Bible says I Peter 2:9, *"But ye are a chosen generation, a royal priesthood, an holy nation, a peculiar people; that ye should shew forth the praises of him who hath called you out of darkness into his marvellous light."*

The Word of God says in Ephesians 6 that the Devil is the god of this world and he has a kingdom of darkness. This means he blinds the minds of people to the truth. When the apostle Paul wrote the church in

Corinth, he said in II Corinthians 4:3, *"But if our gospel be hid, it is hid to them that are lost: in whom the god of this world hath blinded the minds of them which believe not, lest the light of the glorious gospel of Christ, who is the image of God, should shine unto them."*

How many times have you found yourself saying of someone you know or love, "I don't know why he can go on like that. Can't he see?" This is just the problem, he cannot see. He is blinded by Satan.

You may say, "It looks to me as if he could see that he is going to wreck and ruin his life." But he cannot see. He is living in darkness. Some of God's people have stepped into the dark and made wrong decisions because of darkness. God has delivered us from the kingdom of darkness and delivered us into the kingdom of his dear Son, which is a kingdom of light.

In the book of Habakkuk, God compares the darkness of the Babylonians and their lifestyle to the light of the Lord and those who are willing to trust Him. In darkness, they thought they could build up their kingdom by stealing and taking everything they wanted. But God said, "That's not yours!" God said their dark ways were going to be judged, and they were judged.

> *We need to be careful about admiring people who have gotten gain the wrong way. They have God's judgment on their lives.*

THE LUST

In Habakkuk chapter two, God mentions the lust of these people. Remember that the Word of God says the problem is pride. Pride does the same thing for everyone. It tells us that we do not need God. It tells us that we are self-sufficient, that we can direct our own lives and do as we please.

We have an enemy inside of us. We may be attractive on the outside and appear to have everything in order, but on the inside we have an evil beast. We all have an old nature. This old nature is lusting for what is not ours.

Once I took a pastor friend of mine to eat at a cafeteria in the mall. After we finished eating, I said, "There is a place out here where they sell things that you won't believe. The store is called 'The Crystal Vision;' it is of the Devil and none of God's people should ever spend a nickel in it."

We went into the store and I showed him all the books and different things, and then I showed him the rock rack. In this store there were charts and books for each rock. The rocks either contain energy, so they say, or attract energy. If someone needs emotional healing, he can buy a certain kind of rock. For every need, there is a certain stone.

I can just imagine seeing someone that has all kinds of problems wearing a necklace with great big rocks hanging on it. How can sensible people do such a thing? Because they want something for which they are not willing to trust God. There is a lusting of the human heart, wandering in darkness.

By the way, do you know where the first Crystal Vision store ever operated? In Babylon. The Babylonians built the beautiful city of Babylon; inside that city is one of the ancient wonders of the world, the Hanging Gardens. They took pride in how intelligent they were, but they worshipped stones. What we have in our world is nothing more than a revival of Babylonian religion.

Do you know how the "enlightened" Babylonians thought the world got started? They thought that a god and a monster got in a fight. Read it for yourself. Of course, the god defeated the monster and stomped the monster flat and made the earth out of the monster.

Now you will not believe this, but it is true. They thought men got here because every time the god would spit, a man would come up. When a man would spit, a woman would come up. When a woman would spit, an animal would come up.

Now these enlightened Babylonians could build a city sixty miles in circumference. They could build walls around the city that were three hundred feet high and sixty feet wide where chariots could race, and one hundred twenty foot towers every sixty feet on those three hundred foot walls. They had the engineering minds to channel a river through the middle of the city, make a tunnel underneath the river, and barges across the river. They could build beautiful gardens and a city that was a masterpiece in design for all of human history. Yet, these intelligent people were so perverted and away from God that their darkness led them to worship rocks and imagine that the world came into existence through a monster and that people came from spit.

What am I declaring to you? I am declaring to you that men in their degenerate state, with the lust of their evil hearts, apart from God, have no limit to which end they can degenerate.

A few days ago, I was in Dayton, Tennessee, the place of the Scopes Monkey Trial. I thought about the famous trial lawyers, Clarence Darrow and William Jennings Bryan. I thought about my days as a student at the university. I thought about the day I asked my anthropology professor some questions, when he talked to me about the theory of evolution and how we came from monkeys. One day I asked him about monkeys and their tails.

This is a man with a Ph.D., who will not believe the Bible, who will not turn to Jesus Christ by faith, who will not declare this is the truth; he must have his own lustful way. I asked him, "Why don't we still have tails?" He said, "We imagine that one day one of the monkeys was climbing a tree and broke his tail off, and he became the father of men with no tails."

I have a friend who was in an accident and got one of his fingers cut off. If what that professor said is true, when my friend had his next child, it would have been born without a finger.

You see, because the wicked lust of the human heart, men who call themselves so intelligent refuse to allow God to be God and will go to any length to deny that God is God.

The heart lusts for what God does not want us to have, and this lust is founded in pride. The Bible says in Habakkuk 2:5, *"Yea also, because he transgresseth by wine, he is a proud man, neither keepeth at home, who enlargeth his desire as hell, and is as death, and cannot be satisfied."*

We find that he cannot be satisfied. So what does he do? Verses five and six tell us that He *"gathereth unto him all nations, and heapeth unto him all people: shall not all these take up a parable against him, and a taunting proverb against him, and say, Woe to him that increaseth that which is not his!"*

THE LURE

We have an enemy on the inside that refuses to yield to God, so the Devil hangs things out there for us and says, "Come and get it."

The Bible says in James 4:1-2, *"From whence come wars and fightings among you? come they not hence, even of your lusts that war in your members? Ye lust, and have not; ye kill, and desire to have, and cannot obtain: ye fight and war, yet ye have not, because ye ask not."*

Why did these Babylonians take other nations that were not theirs, and why did they heap up things that God did not intend for them to have? Where did these wars come from? Why have men marched into other nations and taken people captive? Why have they done such things?

Here is the point I want to make. There is a lust inside, but there is a lure on the outside. The Devil says, "Come on, this is where it's at; come on, you have never really felt good until you get in this. You've never had this much fun!" The liquor advertisements and other kinds of advertisements promise you, "The night was made for this!" This is the plea of the Devil, the prince of darkness. "Come on, look what we're doing. Look at the fun we're having. Everybody's having a great time. Jump in here with us."

There is a lure by the Devil, a promise that he makes, but he cannot keep the promise he makes. God says, "You want it, but you cannot get it. You cannot obtain it. The satisfaction that your heart longs for cannot be satisfied in those things. It cannot."

Why could Babylon and all the Babylonians not be satisfied with their kingdom, their mighty kingdom, that all the world admired? Why could Nebuchadnezzar not have stayed at home? Why could he not have been content with that beautiful kingdom that he had established? Why could he not have been content? Because he did not live by faith in the true and living God.

The lust of the heart without God says, "I want more and more because nothing satisfies and I have to keep trying something else."

You know the secret, do you not? Nothing satisfies, apart from the Lord Jesus. You can keep chasing after things all your life taking that which is not yours until finally you die and go to hell forever, still wanting more. In hell, the thirst will never be quenched.

The Loss

Notice what God said about them in Habakkuk 2:6-7,

Shall not all these take up a parable against him, and a taunting proverb against him, and say, Woe to him that increaseth that which is not his! how long? and to him that ladeth himself with thick clay! Shall they not rise up suddenly that shall bite thee, and awake that shall vex thee, and thou shalt be for booties unto them?

Notice the question in verse six, *"How long?"* God declared to Habakkuk that there was going to come a time when the Babylonians would reap what they had sown. *"How long?"* Habakkuk did not know how long it would be, but certainly the time would come for Babylon to reap what she had sown. Sometimes we think that we are getting by with things when there is no one else around to see us. But we must never forget there is an omnipresent God who sees and knows all things.

God said in Habakkuk 2:8, *"Because thou hast spoiled many nations, all the remnant of the people shall spoil thee."*

Mighty Babylon, once the greatest kingdom of Mesopotamia, once the mightiest nation on all the earth, today is nothing but a howling wilderness where the city of Babylon once stood.

The historians tell us that no kingdom in all human history rose to such splendor as did Babylon. The capital city of Babylon was located along the Euphrates River. It was a beautiful, magnificent place. The river was canaled so that motes would run around all the city. If you had traveled around the perimeter of Babylon, you would have traveled a distance of nearly sixty miles. Each of its four walls were nearly fifteen miles in length. Within the walls of the city were over eighty gates. The river went under the city walls right through the center of the city. Bridges spanned over the river, and ferries crossed the river. They even had a tunnel underneath the Euphrates River. The walls of the city were over three hundred feet high. Every sixty feet along those walls was a tower that went one hundred and twenty feet higher into the air. It was magnificent!

The dominating king was Nebuchadnezzar who ruled for over sixty years. His palace was six square miles in size. Inside the beautiful palace were the Hanging Gardens of Babylon, called by historians one of the Seven Wonders of the ancient world. Those Hanging Gardens were built for his wife to enjoy.

There was no place in all the world, before or since, that rose to such splendor as did Babylon. But today, the once beautiful Babylon, is covered by water and its ruins can hardly be found.

Notice what the Word of God says in Jeremiah 51:33-37,

> *For thus saith the Lᴏʀᴅ of hosts, the God of Israel; the daughter of Babylon is like a threshingfloor, it is time to thresh her: yet a little while, and the time of her harvest shall come. Nebuchadrezzar the king of Babylon hath devoured me, he hath crushed me, he hath made me an empty vessel, he hath swallowed me up like a dragon, he hath filled his belly with my delicates, he hath cast me out. The violence done to me and to my flesh be upon Babylon, shall the inhabitant of Zion say; and my blood upon the inhabitants of Chaldea, shall Jerusalem say. Therefore thus saith the Lᴏʀᴅ; behold, I will plead thy cause, and take vengeance for thee; and I will dry up her sea, and make her springs dry. And Babylon shall become heaps, a dwellingplace for dragons, an astonishment, and an hissing, without an inhabitant.*

God promised that this magnificent place would become an astonishment because He would destroy it from the face of the earth, and the ruins of the city would not be found. God promised that they would lose all that they had gained.

In Isaiah 13:17-22 God spoke of Babylon,

> *Behold, I will stir up the Medes against them, which shall not regard silver; and as for gold, they shall not delight in it. Their bows also shall dash the young men to pieces; and they shall have no pity on the fruit of the*

womb; their eye shall not spare children. And Babylon, the glory of kingdoms, the beauty of the Chaldees' excellency, shall be as when God overthrew Sodom and Gomorrah. It shall never be inhabited, neither shall it be dwelt in from generation to generation: neither shall the Arabian pitch tent there; neither shall the shepherds make their fold there. But wild beasts of the desert shall lie there; and their houses shall be full of doleful creatures; and owls shall dwell there, and satyrs shall dance there. And the wild beasts of the islands shall cry in their desolate houses, and dragons in their pleasant palaces: and her time is near to come, and her days shall not be prolonged.

God said, "You are going to lose it all." Friends, if we do not learn that we have an enemy that is lying to us and constantly luring us with more and more that will never satisfy, we are going to find out that all we seek to obtain through that lust and lure will be lost. Someday, all will be lost.

We do not have to steal or rob and take that which is not ours. Through Jesus Christ, God has freely given us all we need.

When I was a teenager, I believed the lust lie. I sought after it. I had grown up in it and I wanted it. There was always another one, always something else, always something bigger, brighter, and better to have.

Some days I wondered where the chase would end, and then someone came to me and shared with me the glorious gospel of Jesus Christ. I cannot explain this to you, but when I asked God to forgive my sin and trusted the Lord Jesus as my Savior and gave Him my life, when I yielded my life to Him, it was as though the blinders fell off and I saw the truth. It was as if God pulled the curtain and let me see behind the curtain. The Devil had been laughing at me all the time.

I learned a precious secret. It is found in Romans 8:32, *"He that spared not his own Son* [He gave us the Lord Jesus.] *but delivered him up for us all* [He died for all.] *how shall he not with him also freely give us all things?"*

I found the secret–by trusting the Lord I have gotten to do things I never dreamed I would get to do in life. I have had the opportunity to see things, to be places, to be involved in people's lives, to know a quality of life I never thought was possible. I have an inner peace I have never found anywhere else.

The Lord has freely given us all things, everything we need. We do not have to steal or rob and take that which is not ours. Through Jesus Christ, God has freely given us all we need.

Friend, we must learn that the world is not ours, but the Lord Jesus and all that He has belongs to us. By faith, let us take Him.

"Yea also, because he transgresseth by wine, he is a proud man, neither keepeth at home, who enlargeth his desire as hell, and is as death, and cannot be satisfied."

Habakkuk 2:5

All We Want Is More

For eight years, I had the privilege of pastoring the Madison Avenue Baptist Church of Paterson, New Jersey. The church was located eleven miles from New York City. Quite often I traveled into New York City to visit someone in a hospital or to conduct other matters related to our ministry. Traveling down Westside Drive, along the river, near where the World Trade Center Towers once stood, there was an area filled with sexual perversion. Many times, there were great crowds gathered there along the river. In that area, a sign in big bold letters was positioned so one could read it while passing by. It said, "TOO MUCH IS NEVER ENOUGH." They could never be satisfied, even with what the world says is too much.

As we study this book of the Bible, let us pay close attention to what God tells this prophet as he cries out to the Lord for answers.

The Bible says in Habakkuk 2:9, *"Woe to him that coveteth an evil covetousness to his house, that he may set his nest on high, that he may be delivered from the power of evil!"* Notice also what God says about these people, not only the Babylonians, but all of those who live without the Lord. In the fifth verse of this second chapter, right in the center of the verse, God says, *"...and cannot be satisfied..."*

Can you imagine that people live in such a way that they can never be satisfied? No matter what they have or what they do, they can never be satisfied.

The Babylonians could not be satisfied with their own kingdom. Though they needed nothing else and had conquered much, they could never be satisfied with their accomplishments. When you do not find your satisfaction in the Lord Jesus, absolutely nothing in this world will ever satisfy.

When God's Word comes to the ninth verse of this second chapter and pronounces this judgment upon coveting, He deals with the tenth commandment. The tenth commandment declares God's opposition to the philosophy, "All we want is more. We are never satisfied; all we want is more!"

In the twentieth chapter of the book of Exodus, the Ten Commandments are given. In verse three we have the first commandment, *"Thou shalt have no other gods before me"*; in verse four, the second commandment, *"Thou shalt not make unto thee any graven image"*; in verse seven, number three, *"Thou shalt not take the name of the LORD thy God in vain"*; in verse eight, number four, *"Remember the sabbath day, to keep it holy"*; in verse twelve, number five, *"Honour thy father and thy mother"*; in verse thirteen, number six, *"Thou shalt not kill"*; in verse fourteen, number seven, *"Thou shalt not commit adultery"*; in verse fifteen, number eight, *"Thou shalt not steal"*; in verse sixteen, number nine, *"Thou shalt not bear false witness against thy neighbour."* Commandment number ten is unlike all the other nine. It does not deal with our actions, but our attitude; it does not deal with our deeds, but our desires. It deals with the motive behind breaking all the other nine. In conclusion to these Ten Commandments,

God says, *"Thou shalt not covet."* We are not to live with the idea that we will break all the other nine to get what we want in life. The sin that all of us are guilty of is the sin of breaking the tenth commandment.

The Lord tells us in I Corinthians 12:31 to *"covet earnestly the best gifts."* The word *"covet"* is used in a different sense here. The tenth commandment is speaking of an evil covetousness. This is what God declares the Babylonians are guilty of having.

When a man lives like this, he forgets how brief life is. The brevity of life should stir every one of us to do what we can for Jesus Christ while we can. No matter what you accumulate; no matter what title people use to address you, if you neglect the true God, you are never going to be satisfied. If we live with the philosophy, "All we want is more," we have forgotten that some day we will stand before the Lord.

> *When you do not find your satisfaction in the Lord Jesus, absolutely nothing in this world will ever satisfy.*

Habakkuk's nation was going to be captured by the Babylonians. His heart was broken over the sins of his own people. Yet, God declared in this conversation, how He was going to deal with everyone who had neglected Him. Those of us who know the Lord Jesus as our Savior, who have been made just by the righteousness of Christ being imputed to our account, are to live by faith.

Do you find it difficult to live the Christian life when things that you hoped would turn out a certain way do not turn out that way? Does Christian living still work when things around us are not working?

A pastor friend of mine has several children, but one of them became very ill. I remember when the doctors told my friend that his daughter, who was about nine years old, had something in her brain and she would not live. He had served the Lord faithfully, preaching the Word of God and laboring in the Lord's vineyard. Are things like that supposed to happen to Christians? The Christian life works when nothing else in the world is working.

WHAT WE PURSUE

"Woe to him that coveteth an evil covetousness to his house" (Habakkuk 2:9). Let us think about what we pursue. What are you giving your life to? Everyone of us is on some path trying to get somewhere to accomplish some thing. All of us have a pursuit. We live in a world that bombards us with the idea that we must keep up with someone else, that our pursuit and our precious moments in life should be given to "things." We must place the real value, the high price tag, on what is eternal. The precious, most important things are the eternal things. What we should pursue with our lives is what the Lord Jesus Christ has for us, the true riches. Our goal is God. We must follow after Him.

The brevity of life should stir every one of us to do what we can for Jesus Christ while we can.

The Lord God instructed the prophet to keep his eyes on Him no matter what the Babylonians were going to do. Habakkuk was going to have absolutely nothing left–no house, no land, and no nation. Everything would be taken. It would seem that all was gone, all was wasted, and all was destroyed. In it all, the Lord would remain the same.

All of us give our passion and pursuit to something. We become what we pursue. I see people who have great admiration for others and before long they pick up those peoples' ways. They mimic their speech patterns or the way they walk. They may even comb their hair or wear their clothes a certain way because of who they are passionately pursuing.

The Bible says in Hebrews 13:5-6,

> *Let your conversation be without covetousness; and be content with such things as ye have: for he hath said, I will never leave thee, nor forsake thee. So that we may boldly say, The Lord is my helper, and I will not fear what man shall do unto me.*

God says our pursuit should be Jesus Christ.

Perhaps the most forceful thing in all the Bible about the sin of coveting is found in Colossians 3:5, *"Mortify therefore your members which are upon the earth; fornication, uncleanness, inordinate affection, evil concupiscence, and covetousness, which is idolatry."* Notice God says, *"...covetousness, which is idolatry."* You would not think of going into your home and setting up some little wood or stone idol and looking at it and saying, "I worship you. I adore you. I belong to you." We would not think of finding some image or some picture and putting it in our home and saying, "I worship you. I adore you. I follow you. I give myself to you." But, when we live our lives just to get more, when we follow and pursue other things to the neglect of Jesus Christ, we are saying of those things, "I worship you; I follow you; I adore you; I live for you; I give myself to you." This is why God says that covetousness is idolatry. Allow the Spirit of God to take a inventory of your life and reveal what you are pursuing. Is God your goal?

WHAT WE POSSESS

The Bible says in Habakkuk 2:9, *"Woe to him that coveteth an evil covetousness to his house..."* He is pursuing this for his house. And then God says, *"...that he may set his nest on high."* He pursues this so he can say, "I am the greatest. I am the highest. I am the best." We do not like to admit this, but there is some of this attitude in all of us.

God never called any church to be the greatest church. He never called any preacher to be the greatest preacher. He never called any Christian to be the greatest Christian. He calls all of us to be the best we can be for Him. Living for God has nothing to do with being better, bigger, higher, or greater than someone else.

> *He calls all of us to be the best we can be for Him. Living for God has nothing to do with being better, bigger, higher, or greater than someone else.*

There are many unhappy people behind beautiful walls. There are many unhappy people who drive lovely automobiles. There are many unhappy people who cash large paychecks. There are some happy people who do these things, but if that is what they are depending on for their happiness, they will not be happy for long. What they possess will not bring true happiness.

The Bible says in I Timothy 6:6, *"But godliness with contentment is great gain."* To possess contentment is great gain. Our contentment is found in the Person of Jesus Christ.

WHAT WE PROVE

Each of us is a living lesson; we all prove something. The Bible says that the Babylonians sought to prove that they could be delivered from the power of evil. Yet the judgment of God fell upon them. In one night they found out that with all they had, they still were not safe. God allowed the Medes and Persians to invade them while Belshazzar was drunk in his banquet hall.

ALL WE WANT IS MORE

In Psalm 20:1-9 the Bible says,

> *The LORD hear thee in the day of trouble; the name of the God of Jacob defend thee; send thee help from the sanctuary, and strengthen thee out of Zion; remember all thy offerings, and accept they burnt sacrifice; Selah. Grant thee according to thine own heart, and fulfil all thy counsel. We will rejoice in thy salvation, and in the name of our God we will set up our banners: the LORD fulfill all thy petitions. Now know I that the LORD saveth his anointed; he will hear him from his holy heaven with the saving strength of his right hand. Some trust in chariots, and some in horses: but we will remember the name of the LORD our God. They are brought down and fallen: but we are risen, and stand upright. Save, LORD: let the king hear us when we call.*

God's Word says in verse seven, *"Some trust in chariots, and some in horses: but we will remember the name of the LORD our God."*

In the book of Proverbs, chapter twenty-one, the Word of God says in the last verse, *"The horse is prepared against the day of battle: but safety is of the LORD."* The safest place in all the world is in the will of God.

I am going to live and I am going to die if the Lord Jesus does not return soon, and you are going to live and you are going to die. I want to be alive when He comes, but I may not be. Death is a possibility. The return of the Lord Jesus Christ is a certainty. All of us are going to prove something. We are going to prove by our neglect of the Lord and by our desire just to get more, that more never satisfies; or we are going to prove by yielding our lives to Jesus Christ, that real peace, happiness

The safest place in all the world is in the will of God.

and contentment are found in the Lord. We are going to prove one way or the other.

Remember the parable that the Lord Jesus gave in Luke, chapter twelve. In this chapter you will find that the Lord Jesus was talking to a great group. The Bible says that *"an innumerable multitude"* was gathered around him. He was talking about very serious things and right in the middle of a very serious conversation, one man jumped up and said to the Lord Jesus, "I've got an inheritance coming to me and I want You to help me get it." And the Lord said in Luke 12:15-20,

> *Take heed, and beware of covetousness: for a man's life consisteth not in the abundance of the things which he possesseth. And he spake a parable unto them, saying, The ground of a certain rich man brought forth plentifully: and he thought within himself, saying, What shall I do, because I have no room where to bestow my fruits? And he said, This will I do: I will pull down my barns, and build greater; and there will I bestow all my fruits and my goods. And I will say to my soul, Soul, thou hast much goods laid up for many years; take thine ease, eat, drink, and be merry. But God said unto him, Thou fool, this night thy soul shall be required of thee: then whose shall those things be, which thou hast provided?*

> Death is a possibility. The return of the Lord Jesus Christ is a certainty.

I want to enjoy a certain quality of life and God has blessed me with a quality of life that I never thought I would have. I am not opposed to that. But God opposes living to get. When all we want is more–that is sin.

Think about what we pursue, what we possess, and what we prove. If we live for the world, we prove that the world does not satisfy. If we pursue the Lord Jesus and we possess contentment, we prove that He satisfies. Some people are going to live a long life and prove that the world does not satisfy because they will not live for Christ. Some folks are going to live a long life and prove that Jesus Christ does satisfy because they lived for Him.

However long God lets us live, may our lives prove that Jesus Christ does satisfy.

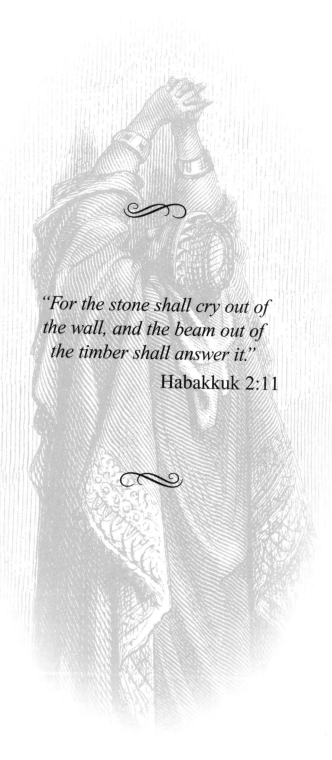

"For the stone shall cry out of the wall, and the beam out of the timber shall answer it."

Habakkuk 2:11

When Stones Speak and Timbers Answer

I n Habakkuk's day, Babylon was the most powerful and most feared nation in all the world. The Lord tells about them in Habakkuk 2:10-14,

> *Thou hast consulted shame to thy house by cutting off many people, and hast sinned against thy soul. For the stone shall cry out of the wall, and the beam out of the timber shall answer it. Woe to him that buildeth a town with blood, and stablisheth a city by iniquity! Behold, is it not of the LORD of hosts that the people shall labour in the very fire, and the people shall weary themselves for very vanity? For the earth shall be filled with the knowledge of the glory of the LORD, as the waters cover the sea.*

Notice what God said in the eleventh verse, *"For the stone shall cry out of the wall, and the beam out of the timber shall answer it."* Let us consider "When Stones Speak and Timbers Answer."

The nation of Babylon had great pride in what it had accomplished. On each of the four sides of the capital city were twenty-five magnificent bronze gates. Through the center of the city ran part of the Euphrates River. There were canals throughout the city, bridges over the river, and even a tunnel running underneath the river. The city was a wonder to behold. Inside, Nebuchadnezzar's queen wanted to see some of the magnificent vegetation from other parts of the world, so Nebuchadnezzar created a garden for her with plants from many other lands.

Babylon had reached its zenith in power and was the strongest nation in all the world, but they had accomplished this by destroying everything in sight and giving absolutely no regard for anyone's welfare, well-being, or safety. God said in Habakkuk 2:12, *"Woe to him that buildeth a town with blood."* God was going to judge Babylon, not because of their position, but because of how they attained that position. God will always judge those who exploit people and use people for personal gain.

As the Babylonians swept through the land, they terrorized people. They would kill the helpless. They would take the bravest soldiers, if captured alive, and make spectacles of them. They would put large hooks in their mouths and lead them around like a child would lead a dog. They would poke out their eyes with flaming torches, and burn and scar their faces, and blind them so they would be led about in mockery. They were known, along with the Assyrians, as the cruelest of all armies that ever marched in the history of mankind. How can human beings, created by God Almighty, become so cruel? They fall so in love with this world and the things of this world that their regard for other human lives completely diminishes.

The Bible says in Habakkuk 2:13, *"Behold, is it not of the LORD of hosts that the people shall labour in the very fire, and the people shall weary themselves for very vanity?"* God says the end of all this Babylonian labor is fire and vanity. Can you imagine spending all your life laboring to build something and never getting any fulfillment out of it? The Bible says they could not be satisfied, no matter how great they became. The Bible says that all their work and labor would be burned up because they had built their city with blood.

God said to Babylon, "Even in all your splendor and all that you take pride in, the stones of your city are going to cry out to you and the timbers that you have used to build it are going to answer them. You are never going to be able to live in peace because everything you have taken to build your empire will be a testimony against you. It cries out that you have sinned against God. You will never be able to enjoy it because you did not achieve it the right way."

God will always judge those who exploit people and use people for personal gain.

We learn a great principle from this verse of Scripture. If you do not get things the right way, you can never enjoy them. If you do not get to where you are going the right way, you will never enjoy being there. If you do not become the kind of person on your way that God desires you to become, you will never be happy when you arrive.

There are people who have lied and stolen and slandered to get to some position in life. They thought when they arrived to that noble, lofty position they would be happy, but it was impossible for them to be happy because what they did along the way to get there testified against them. The stones cried out and the timbers answered!

God says the same thing to us in James 5:1-4,

> *Go to now, ye rich men, weep and howl for your miseries that shall come upon you. Your riches are corrupted, and your garments are moth-eaten. Your gold*

and silver is cankered; and the rust of them shall be a witness against you, and shall eat your flesh as it were fire. Ye have heaped treasure together for the last days. Behold, the hire of the labourers who have reaped down your fields, which is of you kept back by fraud, crieth: and the cries of them which have reaped are entered into the ears of the Lord of sabaoth.

It matters not only what we think we have accomplished, but also what we have done to accomplish it. We imagine that many people in high positions in life are thrilled to be there, but their hearts testify constantly against them if they have done wrong along the way to get to where they are.

If you do not get things the right way, you can never enjoy them.

Though Babylon rose to a great height, greater than all the nations in the world; though they claimed to be the greatest nation in the world; when they entered back into their city, the very stones of the city cried out against them and the timbers answered. They testified that the way they lived was not right.

Did you know that we are going to meet God around every corner? God is going to speak to us in a thousand different ways, through a thousand different things in order to get His message to our hearts.

GLORY CAN TURN INTO SHAME

The Bible says in Habakkuk 2:10, *"Thou hast consulted shame to thy house."*

Their glory turned to shame. There are five woes or judgments that God pronounced on Babylon. The Word of God speaks of the first one in verse six of chapter two, *"Woe to him that increaseth that which is not his!"* Stealing and robbing to get somewhere brings the judgment of God upon us. The second of these woes is found in verse nine, *"Woe to him that coveteth an evil covetousness to his house."* Coveting is saying, "I want more. I am not satisfied with what I have now. I want more." When we desire what is not in God's plan for us to have, we use means that are not pleasing to God to attain such things. God will judge us for this.

Notice the third of these judgments in verse twelve, *"Woe to him that buildeth a town with blood, and stablisheth a city by iniquity!"* This involves exploiting people. Exploiting means to use people to accomplish what we want to accomplish, no matter what it costs those people. How many men have sacrificed their families for their position? How many bosses have sacrificed their employees' happiness to use them only as steps to the top? God says that His judgment is upon this action.

> *Exploiting means to use people to accomplish what we want to accomplish, no matter what it costs those people.*

The Word of God also says in verse fifteen, *"Woe unto him that giveth his neighbor drink, that puttest thy bottle to him, and makest him drunken also, that thou mayest look on their nakedness!"* Drunkenness is always associated with immorality. The judgment of God is upon this.

The Word of God says in verse nineteen, *"Woe unto him that saith to the wood, Awake; to the dumb stone, Arise, it shall teach! Behold, it is laid over with gold and silver, and there is no breath at all in the midst of it."* God pronounces judgment on all idolatry.

These Babylonians were full of glory. They were filled with splendor. King Nebuchadnezzar was on the throne over sixty years, and Babylon was at its highest place in history. In its great glory, the glory of the flesh and the glory of man, all the world trembled at the thought of Babylon. But God said, "Your glory is nothing but shame. You have consulted shame; you have invited shame; you have brought shame into your houses." If we get what we get the wrong way, even though men may praise us, God declares that our glory is nothing but shame. The Bible says in I Peter 1:24, *"For all flesh is as grass, and all the glory of man as the flower of grass. The grass withereth, and the flower thereof falleth away."* The Bible says that all the glory of man is as temporal as the flower of grass that falleth away.

GAIN FOR THEM WAS NOTHING BUT SIN

The Bible says in Habakkuk 2:10, *"Thou hast consulted shame to thy house by cutting off many people, and hast sinned against thy soul."* They gained everything. They ran over everyone. They conquered the mighty nation of Egypt. Even the Assyrian Empire was nothing before the Babylonians. God's people, Judah, were left standing in the geographical bridge through which the Babylonians were to march. No man could stand against them. They were the glory and splendor of the world! They gained it all! They ransacked the temple of God in Jerusalem and took the golden vessels from the house of God back to Babylon to be used in the worship of their heathen gods. God said, "All of your gain has turned into nothing but sin. Because in all of your doing, Babylon, in all of your gaining, you have neglected the true God."

You may be thinking, "I'm so far removed from these awful Babylonians. I'm nothing like them." You had better think again. It is possible to go through life striving to have everything the world has to offer and neglect the only true God.

Ask yourself this question, "Where is God in my life?" God said to these Babylonians, "Your gain is sin because in gaining it, you have neglected your soul."

When Stones Speak and Timbers Answer

No wonder the Lord Jesus said in Mark 8:36, *"For what shall it profit a man, if he shall gain the whole world, and lose his own soul?"* Gain is nothing but sin when we leave God out.

You may say, "I've got a nice place to live." I am happy for you, but that fine home will testify against you if you have neglected God. The walls of that house will cry out against you if you have not made Jesus Christ the Lord of that home.

Far too often houses become vacant because a family has been destroyed by sin. One day that family walked into their house and thought how beautiful it was and how excited they were to have a nice place to live. But then they left God out of the place, and all the gain became nothing but sin. Do you understand this? God says, "You have sinned against your soul because you have accumulated all of this material wealth and you have completely left Me out of it." What at one time seemed so beautiful will testify against you if you leave God out of your life.

We must realize that without Christ in the center of our lives we will never enjoy living. I know many people who started out sincerely wanting to do right, and then they thought that they had one opportunity after another to better themselves. In doing so they neglected the Lord Jesus, His church, and the Bible. They missed the church services to accomplish their goals. When they arrived at the top, they found that they had lost their family, lost their joy, lost their church, lost their church friends, and lost the Christian fellowship they once knew. That kind of success is nothing but sin. Stones will speak and timbers will answer all along the path. It is not worth it when glory turns to shame and our gain cries out against us.

GOD CANNOT BE SILENCED

The Bible says in this eleventh verse, *"For the stone shall cry out of the wall."* The Babylonians said, "We don't worship your God, the God of Judah. We have our own gods. The gods we worship are not your God." God said, "I'll speak through the stones in the walls; I'll cry out and answer in the timbers of your walls! My voice will be heard!" Somehow, someway, somewhere God will speak. God cannot be silenced; His voice will be heard.

When our Lord Jesus was making His triumphant entry into Jerusalem, the people cried out, "Hosanna to the King!" The enemies of Christ wanted His followers to stop speaking. They wanted all the voices of those crying out to be silent. The Bible records the story in Luke 19:37-40,

> *We must realize that without Christ in the center of our lives we will never enjoy living.*

And when he was come nigh, even now at the descent of the mount of Olives, the whole multitude of the disciples began to rejoice and praise God with a loud voice for all the mighty works that they had seen; saying, Blessed be the King that cometh in the name of the Lord: peace in heaven, and glory in the highest. And some of the Pharisees from among the multitude said unto him, Master, rebuke thy disciples. And he answered and said unto them, I tell you that, if these should hold their peace, the stones would immediately cry out.

A young person said to me, "I'm going to get somewhere where God can't get me and my family can't get me and no one else can get me. I'm going so far away from this, I'll never have to listen to it again as long as I live." He should have read the Bible. The Bible says in Psalm 139:1-14,

WHEN STONES SPEAK AND TIMBERS ANSWER

O LORD, thou hast searched me, and known me. Thou knowest my downsitting and mine uprising, thou understandest my thought afar off. Thou compassest my path and my lying down, and art acquainted with all my ways. For there is not a word in my tongue, but, lo, O LORD, thou knowest it altogether. Thou hast beset me behind and before, and laid thine hand upon me. Such knowledge is too wonderful for me; it is high, I cannot attain unto it. Whither shall I go from thy spirit? or whither shall I flee from thy presence? If I ascend up into heaven, thou art there: if I make my bed in hell, behold, thou art there. If I take the wings of the morning, and dwell in the uttermost parts of the sea; even there shall thy hand lead me, and thy right hand shall hold me. If I say, Surely the darkness shall cover me; even the night shall be light about me. Yea, the darkness hideth not from thee; but the night shineth as the day: the darkness and the light are both alike to thee. For thou hast possessed my reins: thou hast covered me in my mother's womb. I will praise thee; for I am fearfully and wonderfully made: marvellous are thy works; and that my soul knoweth right well.

The psalmist said, "I cannot escape God." Neither can we.

When Adam and Eve gave birth to children, one son rose up against the other and killed him. When Abel offered the sacrifice of blood before the Lord, it was pleasing to God. It pointed the way to God and Cain said, "I'll hear none of this! I won't listen to this! You can't preach to me about this! I'll get rid of this! I'll kill my brother and do away with this message about God. I'll kill him and be done with it!"

The Bible says in the book of Genesis that he did kill him. In verse eight of chapter four God's Word says, *"And Cain talked with Abel his brother: and it came to pass, when they were in the field, that Cain rose up against Abel his brother, and slew him. And the LORD said unto Cain, Where is Abel thy brother?"* Cain thought Abel was the only way to hear about God. As soon as Abel was gone, God spoke to him and said, "Where is your brother?" For the rest of Cain's life, when the word "Abel" and the thought of his brother crossed his mind, he was accused of God for his sin. Cain said, *"I know not: am I my brother's keeper: and he said, What hast thou done? the voice of thy brother's blood crieth unto me from the ground."* After God said that to him, that man could never put his foot on the ground again without the ground speaking to him and saying, "Cain, you killed your brother! Cain, you killed your brother!" With every step, "Cain, you killed your brother! You killed your brother!" We cannot get away from God.

> *God cannot be silenced; His voice will be heard.*

The Babylonians said, "We have no God! We don't know God! We'll destroy God's people!" Their glory was turned to shame and their gain became nothing but sin. The God of heaven said, "I will not be silenced. The stones will cry out of your walls and the timbers will answer. You cannot escape Me."

You may say, "I'm going to get a job. I'm going to stay out of church. I'm going to get away. I'm going to get this Christian stuff off my back. I'm going to get rid of this. I'm going a different way." Go ahead and try. Somewhere you will be standing, watching the sun come up, and you will think of the Son of God. Somewhere you will see the leaves blown by the wind and you will remember that there is a Creator who made the trees and the wind that blows. God will get your attention. Perhaps you will walk out some starry night, wondering where in the world your life is headed. You will see all the stars in their beautiful array in the heavens, and you will think that there must be a God somewhere who made them. God will get your attention.

WHEN STONES SPEAK AND TIMBERS ANSWER

Friend, if God can use a rooster and a donkey and many other things in the Bible to speak to people, God can use anything He chooses to speak to you and me. The stones will speak and the timbers will answer. He is inescapable.

A number of years later in Babylon, King Belshazzar sat at a banquet table surrounded by people. The Bible says in the fifth chapter of Daniel that while they sat in a drunken stupor, celebrating their greatness, the hand of God wrote on the wall and told them that their kingdom was destroyed. Literally, the stones and timbers carried God's message to the doomed nation.

God gave to Habakkuk the message that the stones of these Babylonian walls would cry out and the timbers would answer them and accuse them, showing them that they were sinners and that God was going to judge them.

Down south along the Gulf Coast, a girl grew up in a Christian home. She went to church and taught Sunday School. She married someone that knew the Lord and then got into sin. Her marriage broke up. She drifted from God and said, "I'm going to go somewhere where no one will ever know me. No one will know my name. I'll contact my family just when I please." She went to the most populated area of America, and she thought that she was lost in the crowd. She started working in an office by day and took a second job in a clothing store at night. After she had been there for a few years, my wife and I just happened to go into that clothing store at the time she was working her shift. When we finished shopping, we gave her a gospel tract. God said to her, "You can't get away from Me."

When we looked into her face that day, gave her that tract, and spoke to her about the Lord Jesus, it was the first time anyone had spoken to her about God since she had left home as a young lady. She realized that God had trailed her all across America. He had followed her into the most populated area of the country. God brought someone to her to tell her what she thought she would never hear again. He let her know that He knew right where she was and that He loved her.

The end of the story is that she repented of her sin, got right with God, and is serving Christ today with all of her heart. The stones will speak and the timbers will answer. God will never be silenced and He is speaking to you today. Come to Him, trust Him, love Him, and serve Him.

"Woe unto him that giveth his neighbour drink, that puttest thy bottle to him, and makest him drunken also, that thou mayest look on their nakedness!"

Habakkuk 2:15

CHAPTER NINE

What the Lord Says About Liquor

I n the book of Habakkuk, the Lord spoke to the prophet Habakkuk about His judgment upon the nation of Babylon. Babylon was going to come down upon Judah, destroy the land, and carry the people captive. Habakkuk cried out to God and said, "Lord, but they are so wicked! How could this happen?" God declared to Habakkuk that He was going to judge the Babylonians, and He listed five particular areas where His judgment would fall. We come to the fourth of those judgments in Habakkuk 2:15-17,

> *Woe unto him that giveth his neighbour drink, that puttest thy bottle to him, and makest him drunken also, that thou mayest look on their nakedness! Thou art filled with shame for glory: drink thou also, and let thy foreskin be uncovered: the cup of the LORD's right hand shall be turned unto thee, and shameful spewing shall*

be on thy glory. For the violence of Lebanon shall cover thee, and the spoil of beasts, which made them afraid, because of men's blood, and for the violence of the land, of the city, and of all that dwell therein.

Notice what God said in the fifteenth verse, *"Woe unto him that giveth his neighbour drink, that puttest thy bottle to him."*

Let us consider "What the Lord Says About Liquor." Even when people around us are not living for Christ, we can still be victorious through our personal faith in the Lord Jesus Christ. In this world in which we live, standing for the Lord means going against the grain. As we consider what the Lord says about liquor, we realize that God's opinion is not the popular view of our society.

They have entered into the inescapable judgment of God by offering liquor to their neighbor.

In the book of Habakkuk, the Lord said that He was going to judge the Babylonians for their use of alcohol. If the Bible is true and if this statement is truly the Word of God, think of those among athletes, models, and movie actors who have advertised liquor and offered it to the people of the world. God's judgment is already pronounced upon this type of behavior. These people, whom the world considers beautiful, have offered their talents and beauty to advertise for the liquor industry. They are all under the certain judgment of God. It is inescapable. They have entered into the inescapable judgment of God by offering liquor to their neighbor.

If you are wondering why I am so serious about this, I am serious about it because of what the Bible declares and what I have witnessed in the lives of others. The first church I pastored was the Greenback Memorial Baptist Church in Greenback, Tennessee. Early on in that pastorate, as I was returning home in the evening and coming over the hill before turning into the little community of Greenback, I saw that an automobile accident had taken place just moments before I arrived. I stopped my car, got out as quickly as I could, and rushed to the scene of the accident. When I arrived, no one had been moved. Two men had been coming over the hill driving north and had struck a man and his family in an oncoming vehicle. The two men in the automobile were unable to stop their vehicle because they could not control it. They were driving under the influence of alcohol. Oddly enough, they did not sustain any serious injuries, but the family they struck suffered greatly.

I helped load the father into the rescue squad ambulance as he drew his last breath and died. I later had to tell his family that he was dead. I helped load the mother into an ambulance after seeing that her leg was crushed. She was crippled for life. I helped load a little red-headed boy, whose body was cut and his ankle maimed and crushed. He would be crippled for the rest of his life. We pried up the automobile to retrieve a little preschooler from underneath and then reached back under the wreckage and got his leg which had been severed from his body. I carried it in my lap in the ambulance all the way to the hospital. That little boy would have no leg for the rest of his life and would grow up without a father because someone wanted to drink a few beers and have a good time.

DRINKING ALCOHOL CAUSES SUFFERING

The Bible says in Habakkuk 2:15, *"Woe unto him that giveth his neighbour drink, that puttest thy bottle to him, and makest him drunken also, that thou mayest look on their nakedness!"*

The word *"woe"* means judgment and destruction. Drinking alcohol brings suffering. Consider some statistical information I have gathered. One information sheet comes from the third and fourth *Special Reports to the United States Congress on Alcohol and Health.* In this report the medical authorities say that with every drink one shortens his life twenty minutes. They also tell us that there are eleven to seventeen million alcoholics in America. America spends fifty billion dollars a year on alcohol.

We think that we are making money from taxing liquor, that it is a profitable business, but the report to Congress says that alcohol problems cost the American economy an estimated 68.6 billion dollars every year. These are problems that result from people who drink–physical problems, jobs lost, man hours lost, and accidents taking place on the highways. The leading cause of mental retardation among children is alcohol consumption during pregnancy. I say this as kindly as I know how, but a woman is a careless, selfish human being to drink alcohol while carrying a baby.

More than twenty-five thousand people are killed every year on our highways because of alcohol. One person dies every twenty-one minutes in an alcohol-related auto accident. Of course, that does not mean much to us unless someone we know is involved. Eighty-three percent of all fire fatalities are alcohol-related. Fifty to sixty-eight percent of all drownings are alcohol-related. Up to eighty percent of all suicides are alcohol-related. Forty percent of all fatal industrial accidents are alcohol-related. Eighty-six percent of all murders are alcohol-related. Sixty-five percent of all child abuse is alcohol-related. This same report says that two hundred thousand Americans die each year, either because of their own consumption of alcohol or someone else's consumption of alcohol. This information can be obtained by anyone who is interested in knowing the truth.

Another report entitled, "The Truth About Beer," is provided by the United Tennessee League because some people think it is all right to have a few beers.

Approximately fifty percent of all teenagers have tried beer before they enter high school. Ninety percent of all high school graduates have used beer. Peer pressure is great to join the crowd and have a couple of beers. Eighty percent of the teenagers who drink today indicated that their friends also drink.

Television commercials present a very glamorous picture of beer drinking. Endorsements by highly recognizable former athletes make beer drinking appear to be the macho thing to do. These commercials show young people enjoying the 'good life' with a beer or other alcoholic beverage in hand. In some commercials, beautiful models endorse beer and thus the sex appeal angle is introduced: 'If you want to get a pretty girl, drink a beer.' Television programs consistently depict the drinking of alcohol as an integral part of an attractive and successful life, and in many programs, alcohol is presented as a way of coping with the problems of life.

And in case you do not know the facts about beer, the article says,

The alcohol contained in beer is grain alcohol, chemically known as ethyl alcohol. The percentage of alcohol in beer ranges from approximately three percent to eight percent. This may not seem like much alcohol; however, a twelve-ounce can or bottle of beer contains a half ounce of alcohol. This is the same amount of alcohol that you would obtain from other drinks such as a glass of wine filled with natural wine, an average cocktail, an average highball, an average martini, or a shot of one hundred proof whiskey. Approximately sixty percent of the alcohol consumed in the United States is from beer. Clearly, beer is the beverage of choice by Americans. Alcohol is a very powerful drug to which the body can quickly develop both a psychological and physiological dependence. There are at least eleven million alcoholics and perhaps as many as seventeen million alcoholics in America. Many hundreds of thousands of them are teenagers.

"One out of every ten drinkers becomes addicted to alcohol. Statistics indicate that one out of every two people will be involved in an alcohol-related accident in their lifetime." You may say, "It's none of my business." If you have never taken a drink, it is still your business because half of us are going to be hurt by someone who is drinking.

Alcohol is involved in approximately sixty percent of all highway fatalities. In the United States alone, over twenty-five thousand people die and seven hundred fifty thousand injuries occur on American highways each year because of alcohol. Three quarters of a million people are injured because of alcohol each year in America. Three people are killed and eighty people are injured by alcohol every hour in America. On a typical weeknight, one out of every ten drivers is driving under the influence of alcohol.

And one article said, "There are certain hours during the day when they have proven that not only one out of every ten, but three out of every ten drivers are under the influence of alcohol."

Many say that liquor is a disease. Someone has said, "If liquor is a disease, it's the only disease that requires a license to propagate it. It's the only disease that's bottled and sold. It's the only disease that requires outlets to spread it. It's the only disease that is spread by advertising."

Does it do something to you when you see athletes getting their bodies in tremendous condition and then to see that the sporting events are sponsored, for the most part, by beer companies?

A former Prime Minister of England, William Gladstone, frequently distributed this article to his friends:

Drunkenness expels reason, drowns the memory, distempers the body, diminishes strength, inflames the blood, causes internal and external wounds; it's a witch to the senses; a devil to the soul; a thief to the purse; a beggar's companion; a wife's woe, and children's sorrow.

I remember the night when my youngest son graduated from our Christian school as valedictorian of his class. I was so grateful to the Lord for him. But the night that I watched him graduate, I could not help but recall that we had a lovely couple in the first church I pastored, who had a son the same age as my youngest son. They were in school together. They had planned to graduate the same night. But their son did not graduate. Their son, a few weeks before graduation, took a friend home and was coming back to his home to be in at the proper time that his parents had allotted for him. A man and a woman in an automobile, who had already taken their clothes off in a drunken stupor, were driving down the highway on the wrong side of the road and crashed into the automobile driven by this young man. They killed him instantly. The drunken driver never knew that he struck my young friend.

Drinking liquor causes suffering. The world is suffering for many reasons, but one of the biggest reasons is beverage alcohol–beer, wine coolers, liquor, and all the rest. God is against it because it causes suffering. It could be you or one of your precious children that is the next to be killed.

DRINKING ALCOHOL CAUSES SHAME

The Bible says in Habakkuk 2:15, *"Woe unto him that giveth his neighbour drink, that puttest thy bottle to him and makest him drunken also, that thou mayest look on their nakedness!"*

God associates drinking with immorality. He ties the two together. If you ever notice the beer commercials, they are promoting an immoral lifestyle. They say, "Live it up!" And the beautiful young bodies that you see will not remain young and beautiful forever because drinking liquor will cause shame.

I noticed, in my reading, that a famous actor who portrays a constant drinker and philosopher on a television sitcom has had himself admitted into an alcoholics' treatment center. Though he portrays a character that promotes drinking every week on television, he has had to admit himself into an alcoholics' treatment center and has tried to commit suicide on a number of occasions while in that center. I am not against that man, but I am against his sin and what he promotes. If anyone should see it, he should see it. I could go down a list of famous people who have either overdosed, killed themselves, or wrecked and ruined their lives because of their drinking or substance abuse. Drinking brings shame.

Have you ever seen a drunken woman? I remember from my childhood seeing drunken women. Everything that was decent and holy about life was shamefully disgraced as something beautiful turned into something animal-like. These women had no regard for what they did; they had no shame in showing their bodies or using filthy language because of drinking liquor.

The Word of God says in Habakkuk 2:16, *"Thou art filled with shame for glory: drink thou also, and let thy foreskin be uncovered: the cup of the LORD's right hand shall be turned unto thee, and shameful spewing shall be on thy glory."*

What does the last part of verse sixteen mean? It literally means that they would be vomiting on their own glory. He said, "Mighty Babylon, greater than all, you will be vomiting on your own glory." If you will remember from the reading of God's Word in Daniel chapter five, one night the leaders of Babylon were in a drunken stupor and fell to the Medes and Persians.

Many a man has started out handsome, robust, and strong, and many a young lady has started out looking beautiful. Somehow they found their way into a singles' bar or some "club," and the Devil lied to them until everything good was gone. No honor was left. Their honor was given to the cruel, and now all that is left is shame.

WHAT THE LORD SAYS ABOUT LIQUOR

I know men and women of means who have destroyed their health; who started drinking with family as young people, and today they are drunks. Even with all the wealth they possess, they cannot regain what they have lost. Their lives are covered with shame because of drinking.

Heed this warning that the Lord gives us in Hosea 4:6, *"My people are destroyed for lack of knowledge: because thou hast rejected knowledge, I will also reject thee, that thou shalt be no priest to me: seeing thou hast forgotten the law of thy God, I will also forget thy children."*

You may need to share this with someone someday because God will use His Word to speak to that person. God is speaking here about the leadership of Israel and what happened to them. He rejects them, and I want you to notice why. The Bible continues in verses seven through eleven,

> *As they were increased, so they sinned against me: therefore will I change their glory into shame. They eat up the sin of my people, and they set their heart on their iniquity. And there shall be, like people, like priest: and I will punish them for their ways, and reward them their doings. For they shall eat, and not have enough: they shall commit whoredom, and shall not increase: because they have left off to take heed to the LORD. Whoredom and wine and new wine take away the heart.*

God says the entire problem came with whoredom and drinking, and He had to reject His own people.

The Bible says in Isaiah 28:7,

> *But they also have erred through wine, and through strong drink are out of the way; the priest and the prophet have erred through strong drink, they are swallowed up of wine, they are out of the way through strong drink; they err in vision, they stumble in judgment.*

Lord, Send a Revival

In Proverbs 20:1 the Bible says, *"Wine is a mocker, strong drink is raging: and whosoever is deceived thereby is not wise."* You do not know what you have your hands on when you hold a bottle of beer. You do not know what you have your hands on when you hold a glass of wine. You may say, "I know people who can handle it." No, you do not, friend. It just looks as if they can now.

You may ask, "What about wine?" Go with me to New York City, where I spent eight years ministering to people, or any other major city in America, and I will show you the people whose minds are gone. What do we call them? We call them "winos." Why are they called winos? Because the cheap wine that they drink destroys more of the brain cells than any other beverage alcohol. Wine is a mocker. This is what the Bible says.

In Proverbs 23:19-35 the Bible says, *"Hear thou, my son, and be wise, and guide thine heart in the way. Be not among winebibbers; among riotous eaters of flesh."* This means if you have gotten into the company of drinkers, you had better find another crowd.

"For the drunkard and the glutton shall come to poverty: and drowsiness shall clothe a man with rags. Hearken unto thy father that begat thee, and despise not thy mother when she is old." "Those old people don't know what they are talking about!" They do know what they are talking about!

> *Buy the truth, and sell it not; also wisdom, and instruction, and understanding. The father of the righteous shall greatly rejoice: and he that begetteth a wise child shall have joy of him. Thy father and thy mother shall be glad, and she that bare thee shall rejoice.*

No mother and father rejoices when their children are in sin, destroying their lives. The Bible says,

> *My son, give me thine heart, and let thine eyes observe my ways. For a whore is a deep ditch; and a*

*strange woman is a narrow pit. She also lieth in wait as
for a prey, and increaseth the transgressors among men.
Who hath woe? Who hath sorrow? Who hath
contentions? Who hath babbling? Who hath wounds
without cause? Who hath redness of eyes? They that
tarry long at the wine; they that go to seek mixed wine.
Look not thou upon the wine when it is red, when it
giveth his colour in the cup, when it moveth itself aright.*

Have you seen the wine-tasters move the wine around and talk about
the body and the fragrance of the wine and how beautiful it is. The
Bible says not to look at it because,

*At the last it biteth like a serpent, and stingeth like an
adder. Thine eyes shall behold strange women, and thine
heart shall utter perverse things. Yea, thou shalt be as he
that lieth down in the midst of the sea, or as he that lieth
upon the top of a mast. They have stricken me, shalt thou
say, and I was not sick; they have beaten me, and I felt
it not: when shall I awake? I will seek it yet again.*

How pitiful! People wake up after being affected by liquor, but when
they wake up they get another drink.

I have seen people beautifully dressed enter into a place and come
out acting like, excuse me, the worse kind of harlot that ever lived.
What changed their behavior? Alcohol. I have seen mighty strong men
brought down by alcohol. Drinking brings suffering; drinking brings
shame; but, drinking liquor can be stopped.

DRINKING ALCOHOL CAN BE STOPPED

The Lord Jesus Christ can enable a person to stop drinking. This is not
a matter that one can simply fight his way through; he must have God's

power. You may say, "I'm going to turn over a new leaf. I'm going to give up the booze. I'll clean out my refrigerator; I'll never take another drink." That will not do it. It is not just turning from the evil; it is turning to the Lord that we need.

> *Every victory in life is won by living consciously in the presence of Jesus Christ.*

I would to God that every man, woman, boy and girl in the world would say, "I'll give my life to the Lord Jesus. I'll ask Him to forgive my sin and by faith trust Him as my Savior." Are you a Christian? Are you truly a Christian? Then may everyone of us say, "By the grace of God, we will live for Christ." If you do not know Him as your Savior, you should trust Him now. Ask Him to forgive your sin and be your Savior. Living for Christ is a daily matter. You will be strengthened day by day, and with each passing day, God will help you to be stronger to resist temptation. It will be a daily matter, but you can stop.

Every evil in our lives should be treated as if we are living with the Devil himself, and we should say, "God, help me! I won't bring this Devil into my life anymore! God, help me." Call it "sin" like it is. Call it sin and go to Christ and ask Him to help you. Ask Him to forgive you and help you and He will. Every victory in life is won by living consciously in the presence of Jesus Christ.

This is not just about drinking liquor. The Lord Jesus loves you and will forgive you for everything you have ever done and come and live in your life. He will give you the Holy Spirit to empower you to do what is right if you will simply trust Him. No one can trust Him for you. Others can pray for you and they can love you, but you must give your heart to Him. May God help you to do this today.

*"Woe unto him that saith
to the wood, Awake; to the
dumb stone, Arise, it shall teach!
Behold, it is laid over with gold
and silver, and there is no breath
at all in the midst of it."*

Habakkuk 2:19

Chapter Ten

Calling on Gods That Cannot Answer

merica has become a garden of strange gods. We are becoming increasingly aware of this. Our land is filled with strange gods. It has been reported that as many as eight hundred non-conventional religions are now being practiced in America. We have moved from an age of materialistic thinking, where all that mattered was money and materialistic gain, into an age of mysticism. The materialism of the West has been met by the mysticism of the East. We act as if something new is taking place, so much so that we have identified it as the New Age. Actually, it is nothing but a revival of old heathenism.

As we have traveled through the book of Habakkuk together, we have noticed that God pronounced judgment upon certain things that existed in the lives of the Babylonians. Remember that Habakkuk stood on the eve of the captivity of his nation. His name, *Habakkuk*, means "one who embraces." He embraced the Lord and sought the answer from God. He said to the Lord that the people of Judah had forsaken God. Habakkuk knew that they should be judged, and he asked the Lord how long He would allow them to continue in sin. God spoke to Habakkuk and said, "I'm going to send the Babylonians to judge them." Habakkuk's heart was so stirred. He said, "How can this be? They are wicked. How can You use them to judge us? Though we are wicked, we are not as wicked as they." God declared to Habakkuk that He would use the Babylonians to come down and take the nation of Judah captive, but He would also judge Babylon. In the second chapter He gave those judgments. In chapter two, verse six, He said, *"Woe to him that increaseth that which is not his!"* In verse nine He said, *"Woe to him that coveteth an evil covetousness."* In verse twelve He said, *"Woe to him that buildeth a town with blood."* In verse fifteen He said, *"Woe unto him that giveth his neighbour drink."* Then the Lord said in verses eighteen through twenty,

> *What profiteth the graven image that the maker thereof hath graven it; the molten image, and a teacher of lies, that the maker of his work trusteth therein, to make dumb idols? Woe unto him that saith to the wood, Awake; to the dumb stone, Arise, it shall teach! Behold, it is laid over with gold and silver, and there is no breath at all in the midst of it. But the LORD is in his holy temple: let all the earth keep silence before him.*

In this fifth judgment, God pronounced to Babylon, *"Woe unto him that saith to the wood, Awake; to the dumb stone, Arise, it shall teach!"* Notice, also, that God declared, *"There is no breath at all in the midst of it."* I want us to study this portion of Scripture and consider this subject, "Calling on Gods That Cannot Answer."

So many of us are trusting in things that cannot help us. No matter how sincere our confidence and trust in those things may be, no matter how long we place our trust in those things, we are calling on gods that can never answer.

CALLING ON GODS THAT CANNOT ANSWER

Recently, I boarded a plane to fly to a speaking appointment and I took the flight magazine, as I often do, just to browse through it briefly. This magazine was the *American Way* magazine, which is the flight magazine for American Airlines. The feature story in this particular magazine had to do with some ancient practice to help people. I read the article and it began with these comments:

> Consider this event: a New York book editor turns his desk and computer so he faces the door, instead of having his back to the door. In a matter of months, this editor is promoted. Consider this event: a vice president at Manhattan's Morgan Bank, whose desk is near the managing editor, places a crystal at an angle on his desk. He suddenly feels more confident. Consider this event: the president of Vintage Northwest, a Seattle company that promotes Washington state wines, moved his office desk from a classroom style alignment to a more slanted position. Within a month, business improves substantially. Are these coincidents? No, not at all.

An ancient practice based on the idea that the placement of buildings, doors, furniture, even grave sights can bring good fortune has long been used in the Orient. Now it is catching on in the corporate offices of America. The experts who promote this ancient ritual have us consider the shape of buildings and their physical surroundings. Then they offer advice on everything from the placement of windows to the positioning of doors. With that, the client is assured of the building's ability to attract prosperity and to keep bad spirits away. In that article they said that some of the promoters of this particular ancient ritual are advising many of the Fortune Five Hundred Companies in America. You would be startled to know how many business executives have a crystal on their desk which brings to them, so they say, power. They are saying, "Dumb stone, Arise and speak." They are saying to some image, "I'm going to trust you to bring prosperity to me and to keep evil away." While we are sleeping in this country, strange gods are moving in. They are gods that cannot answer. Men are calling on them, but they cannot answer to meet the need of the human heart.

The Bible says in Habakkuk 2:19, *"Woe unto him* [The judgment of God is upon him.] *that sayeth to the wood, Awake; to the dumb stone, Arise, it shall teach!"*

There are more and more places in nearly every city in this country where one can buy a stone, thinking that stone can help him in some way. One of the biggest things happening on our academic campuses today is the worship of stones and pet rocks. Some people even sleep under a pyramid image for power. We have become like the ancient Babylonians, willing to trust in everyone but God for what we need. As America becomes a nation of the deceived, we have become a people who are calling on gods that cannot answer.

According to a recent religious poll, eighty percent of the American population today identifies with some religious group. This is the highest figure in the modern history of America. Eighty percent of America is identified with some religious group, but eighty percent of those people say that Jesus Christ is not fully sufficient for salvation.

The Lord Jesus said, *"I am the way, the truth, and the life: no man cometh unto the Father, but by me"* (John 14:6). Do you believe this, or do you reject this? We can have children in our public schools today who practice meditation and chant names of Hindu gods, but they cannot read the Bible and pray. We can have people come into corporate places and lecture on how office managers can meditate and teach their employees to meditate and call on heathen gods, but no one dares to mention the name of Jesus Christ. We can have alluring television commercials on the science of dynamics and scientology and promote what these things can do to improve life and business and bring world peace in a global community, but we dare not speak about the Lord Jesus.

CALLING ON GODS THAT CANNOT ANSWER

This is not India and the land of the Hindus. This is not Japan and the land of the multiple gods. This is America where we stand and say, "I pledge allegiance to the flag of the United States of America and to the republic for which it stands, one nation under God, indivisible, with liberty and justice for all." America has become a garden of strange gods. Our boys and girls and men and women are foolish enough to call on gods that cannot answer. God says His judgment is upon this.

Jesus Christ is truth, and He is the only way to heaven. If you have not trusted Him, you cannot get to heaven. What God is dealing with, in this fifth pronouncement of judgment upon Babylon, is idolatry. Idolatry, simply defined, is worshipping the creature instead of the Creator. It is worshipping what has been created instead of the One who created it, God Almighty. Our country is full of idolatry.

When the Lord pronounced judgment upon the nation of Babylon, notice what He said in Isaiah 47:11, *"Therefore shall evil come upon thee; [speaking to Babylon] thou shalt not know from whence it riseth..."* If you know about the destruction of Babylon, you know that the Medes and Persians diverted the Euphrates River and came into the banquet hall where Belshazzar had a feast with one thousand of his lords and drank wine before the thousand. In their drunken stupor they did not know what was happening until the hand of God wrote on the wall, *"Thou art weighed in the balances, and art found wanting"* (Daniel 5:27). God said that they would not even know where their judgment was coming from. The Lord continued in Isaiah 47:11, *"...and mischief shall fall upon thee; thou shalt not be able to put it off: and desolation shall come upon thee suddenly, which thou shalt not know. Stand now with thine enchantments."* After God said that He would judge them and bring them down, He told them to call on their enchantments, their strange gods.

Jesus Christ is truth, and He is the only way to heaven.

The Bible says in Isaiah 47:12-13,

> *Stand now with thine enchantments, and with the multitude of thy sorceries, wherein thou hast laboured from thy youth; if so be thou shalt be able to profit, if so be thou mayest prevail. Thou art wearied in the multitude of thy counsels. Let now the astrologers, the stargazers, the monthly prognosticators, stand up, and save thee from these things that shall come upon thee.*

God says, "How is the horoscope going to help you now? How are the stargazers going to help you now?" When people try to find out what the stars say so they can know what to do, they are doing the same thing the Babylonians did. This is right out of hell. We live in a land where people have turned from God. They have created a vacuum in their lives and have opened up themselves to all kinds of false gods. We live in a land that is full of pantheism. Pantheism is the belief that god is in everything and in everybody, and ultimately man is god.

> *The passion of every true believer in Jesus Christ should be to glorify God.*

The Babylonians made a god of everything in sight. I never thought I would live in a day when I would walk into a place and people would have rocks on their desks and think a rock is going to deliver them.

You say, "I don't have stones on my desk." Let me ask you a question, "Are you calling on gods that cannot answer you?"

In Psalm 115:1 the Bible says, *"Not unto us, O Lord, not unto us, but unto thy name give glory, for thy mercy, and for thy truth's sake."* The passion of every true believer in Jesus Christ should be to glorify God.

The Bible says in Psalm 115:2, *"Wherefore should the heathen say, Where is now their God?"* I want you to stop and notice that this world, this wicked world in which we live, is saying to the church, "Where is your God? What has He done? What has He accomplished? What can He do? Who is your Savior? Where is your God?" Most of us who are saved live such weak, anemic Christian lives that the world never sees the Lord Jesus in us. The Lord declares in Psalm 115:3-9,

> *But our God is in the heavens: he hath done whatsoever he hath pleased. Their idols are silver and gold, the work of men's hands. They have mouths, but they speak not: eyes have they, but they see not: they have ears, but they hear not: noses have they, but they smell not: they have hands, but they handle not: feet have they, but they walk not: neither speak they through their throat. They that make them are like unto them; so is every one that trusteth in them. O Israel, trust thou in the LORD: he is their help and their shield.*

We need a revival in our land, a revival of old-fashioned, Bible-believing, Christian living, where people honor the Lord and let God be God of their lives.

We need a revival in our land, a revival of old-fashioned, Bible-believing, Christian living, where people honor the Lord and let God be God of their lives. I am thoroughly convinced that the reason our country is in such pitiful shape is not because the gods of the East have been able to make such inroads, but because the true God has not been allowed to work in the lives of Christians. We create a vacuum for these heathen gods to rush in. The reason false gods flourish is that we are not on fire for the Lord.

When you read the Old Testament, read about the pagan temples being filled and the heathen rejoicing in their gods and glorifying their gods for giving victory. If you read in the Old Testament and find out when that happened, you will see that it was because God's people were not living for their Lord and giving glory to Him. This should be a clarion call to everyone of us. If you are saved, you should begin to live as a Christian and be thoroughly dedicated to Jesus Christ. If you are not saved, you should realize that the Lord Jesus Himself said the clearest thing possible about salvation when He said, *"I am the way, the truth, and the life: no man cometh unto the Father, but by me"* (John 14:6).

THE TEST OF DEVOTION

Where are our gods today? Let us take a test. Let us take the test of devotion. The test of devotion has to do with what we are working for. Can you define what you are working for? You may say, "I'm working to get money." It should go further than that. What do you plan to do with that money? As Christians, we should use our money to honor the Lord, to honor God's work, to live the right kind of life and provide for our families. If to attain money is the goal, then your devotion is to a god that cannot answer. Our devotion should be given to the only true and living God.

THE TEST OF DELIGHT

Let us take the test of delight. Delight has to do with what pleases us. God's Word says in Psalm 37:4, *"Delight thyself also in the LORD; and he shall give thee the desires of thine heart."* The only way some people can be happy is to be involved in the things of this world. They run everywhere to one thing after another, partying night and day or getting involved with things they should never participate in. Their delight is constantly in something other than Jesus Christ. If this is true in your life, face the facts that you are an idol worshipper. You have made a god of those things you pursue for your delight. Many of these things may be good, but they were never meant to be gods. Our delight should be in the Lord Jesus Christ.

THE TEST OF DEPENDENCE

Let us take the test of dependence. On what do we depend? Our faith and confidence should be in the Lord. We should believe that God is able to do *"exceeding abundantly above all that we ask or think"* (Ephesians 3:20). If we are trusting in men to manipulate, to work, to scheme, to connive, to plan and get things done, we have made an idol out of someone because we are not depending on the Lord Jesus Christ.

THE TEST OF DECISION

Let us take the test of decision. What do we depend on to guide us? I must be guided by the Word of God and by the indwelling Holy Spirit. If you read the horoscope, you are giving the Devil an opportunity to guide you. You are making an idol out of it. A Christian should be guided in his decisions by the Word of God and the indwelling Holy Spirit. Are you an idol worshipper when it comes to what guides you? Do not read the stars, read the Bible.

THE TEST OF DESTINY

Let us take the test of destiny. What are you looking forward to? Is heaven on your mind? Is the coming of Jesus Christ on your mind? My destiny is settled. My destiny is heaven. My destiny is Christ. My destiny is to be with Him and to be like Him. If I am only living for and looking forward to other things short of that, I have made an idol out of those things. It is a very simple test to take. We are either worshipping Jesus Christ or we are calling on gods that cannot answer.

One day I walked into a pastor's office and we talked together about the things of the Lord. He showed me a picture on a cabinet above his desk. I want you to try to fasten this in your mind for a moment. It was a picture of a beautiful eighteen-year-old girl, as normal looking as you would ever imagine anyone would look. He said, "That's my daughter. That's my pride and joy. If I had written a request for the kind of girl I wanted, she met all the requirements. She made me happy; she honored the Lord; she played the piano for us; she made plans to go to a Christian college. She planned to serve God with all her life and had looked forward to this since her earliest remembrances." He said, "That's the kind of girl every daddy wants his daughter to be. A few months ago she got headaches and we took her to the doctor and found out that she has a malignant brain tumor. The tumor is inoperable; there is nothing we can do. She has had so many radiation treatments that many of her brain cells have been destroyed and she doesn't look like that anymore, and the thing that is killing us is she doesn't behave as she once behaved. She says things and does things that she never would have said or done before. It doesn't look like she is going to get well. She won't take her medication. She won't comply with anything her mother and I want her to do. I'm trying to serve as a pastor and trying to serve as the president of a college, and this is the biggest thing on my heart and mind." He said, "The only thing I know to do is simply trust the Lord." We prayed together and we trusted the Lord with her life.

If Jesus Christ is worthy to call on in a crisis, He should also be called on every day even when we do not face the great crisis.

The day will come in your life when something will happen and things that you thought were important will not be important at all. The only thing that will matter is that you can reach God. This is why God said to these Babylonians, "You go on your way, you do as you please, but when the judgment falls, call your astrologers and your stargazers and your prognosticators in and see what they can do for you then."

Friend, let me tell you something that I hope you understand and never forget as long as you live. If Jesus Christ is worthy to call on in a crisis, He should also be called on every day even when we do not face the great crisis. May God help us to call on the only God who can answer. He is none other than the Lord Jesus Christ.

"O LORD, I have heard thy speech, and was afraid: O LORD, revive thy work in the midst of the years, in the midst of the years make known; in wrath remember mercy."

Habakkuk 3:2

CHAPTER
ELEVEN

The Heart Cry for Revival

T he greatest need of this hour is the need for revival. It is our responsibility to evangelize the world. We must take the message of Jesus Christ to every creature. World evangelism is not a man-made idea; it is not a marketing method someone came up with to sell religious material. It is the command of Jesus Christ to go *"into all the world, and preach the gospel to every creature"* (Mark 16:15). But evangelism is not revival.

A revival involves the people of God. Evangelism is God's people telling lost people about Christ. Revival is God's people getting their hearts stirred. A revival is a new beginning of obedience to God. We need a new beginning of obedience to God.

The Bible says in Habakkuk 3:1-2, *"A prayer of Habakkuk the prophet upon Shigionoth. O LORD, I have heard thy speech, and was afraid: O LORD, revive thy work in the midst of the years, in the midst of the years make known; in wrath remember mercy."*

LORD, SEND A REVIVAL

Notice that Habakkuk declared, *"O LORD, revive thy work."* Let us consider "The Heart Cry for Revival." We must understand from the very beginning that a revival is between an individual and God. If we do not have a revival, it is our fault, not God's. It is a personal matter. I can have a revival whether the church I am a part of experiences revival or not. Revivals do not come first to churches, they come first to individuals, and then, they may spread through churches.

GOD DESIRES TO WORK THROUGH US

Remember that the prophet Habakkuk was standing on the eve of the captivity of his nation. The Babylonians were about to come down and take captive the little nation of Judah. It may have been a tiny nation as far as world affairs and the population were concerned, but nothing could be more important than the people and the place where God had chosen to work. To those people and through those people, God desired to make Himself known to the rest of the world.

In our churches God wants to make Himself known to us and through us to all those around us. This will not happen unless we have a revival.

REVIVAL IS OUR ONLY HOPE

The only hope for our country is revival. If we believe our only hope is revival and the only people that can have a revival are God's people, then we, who know the Lord, hold the key of hope.

I certainly do not believe that revival will come to a church that does not believe the Bible. I do not believe revival will come to a people who do not know the Lord. Dr. Vance Havner, who is now in heaven, said, "You can't have 'revival' until you have 'vival.'" This means you must have life before that life can be revived. This is what a revival is all about.

Habakkuk faced a serious situation. His nation was going to be led captive. The mind of God was not going to be changed. This calamity was inescapable. Judah was going into captivity and the prophet said, "I've come now to believe that the only thing we can ask God for is revival."

The judgment of God upon our country is inevitable; it is inescapable. We will be judged for our sins, and the only hope that we have is revival. Let us pray, *"In wrath remember mercy."*

REVIVAL MEANS GREATER DEVOTION TO CHRIST

All believers know that we need a higher level of devotion to Jesus Christ. When a revival comes, people will be willing to serve the Lord because they are devoted to Christ.

REVIVAL INCREASES THE LABOR FORCE FOR CHRIST

We need more people involved in the work of the Christian ministry. We need more people witnessing, more people praying, and more people faithfully attending church. We need more people involved in the work force of every church.

When I was just a boy, living at home, my mother was trying to rear four children, and each of us had responsibilities. I had to do housework. We almost always lived in town, so we had very little yard. I had the responsibility of sweeping the yard. Did you ever sweep the yard? This is what you do when you do not have grass; you sweep the yard. It may sound funny, but it is true. We did not have grass, so we swept the yard and we watered the yard, not for the grass, but to keep the dust down. If we put too much water on it, we would get mud. My mother would come out and say, "You're not paying attention! You've got a mud hole out there now. You are going to track it inside, and then you will have to clean the house again."

She taught me how to sweep, how to mop, and how to wash. I went to the laundry mat. We did not own a washing machine and dryer. The local laundry mat had huge dryers and we could throw everything in them. We just placed two dimes in the washing machine, put in washing powders, and got it all going. Then we took the wash out and carried it over to the big dryer. Mother also taught me how to fold the clothes. I took the clothes to wash in large paper bags, and when I finished washing I had to fold them and place them back into those bags in order to carry them home. My mother could not get it all done because she was working ten to twelve hours a day. I had to do it. It was my job.

She taught me how to mop the floor and how to wash dishes. I was taught to rinse the dishes in very hot water so that they felt clean when I got through with them. There was work for every child to do.

In the family of God everyone should assume part of the workload. We need more people helping with the workload. Some people who once served no longer serve. A revival will cause more people to get under the load.

Revival Causes Greater Interest in the Lord's Work

The longer I live, the fewer things I can get involved in. I am very happy, and I enjoy my life, but I must narrow my interest. As Christians, we cannot do all we once did. We cannot behave frivolously. We must think, "What does God want me to do? I must do God's work." We must narrow our interest. A revival will take care of this. We must learn to eliminate good things for the best things.

Revival Brings Zeal for the Lord

We must have the zeal to take advantage of the unparalleled opportunities that are given to us today. More doors are open today than ever before. We need zeal to take advantage of all the opportunities that God is giving us in this hour. If we have revival, it will bring about a deep dissatisfaction, a wrestling with God, a discontentment with self.

Just before the 1900's there were very few Americans on the mission fields around the world. A man named D. L. Moody had a meeting in Northfield, Massachusetts, at the urging of some of his friends. They asked him to speak to students who came to that particular meeting. Students were there from eighty-six different colleges. It was not really planned as a meeting about missions, but it turned into a missions meeting because one of the speakers had a heavy heart for missions. The mission emphasis came out of the revival that took place. During the next twenty to twenty-five years, over ten thousand Americans volunteered for the mission field as a result of that meeting. From very few to over ten thousand in a few short years went to the fields of the world because of one revival meeting. There is a God in heaven who sees the needs of our country and other nations around the world and is waiting for His people to wake up and do His work before the trumpet sounds and Jesus Christ comes again.

> *The judgment of God upon our country is inevitable; it is inescapable. We will be judged for our sins, and the only hope that we have is revival. Let us pray, "In wrath remember mercy."*

I have been to Mount Hermon in Northfield on a number of occasions and have read the inscription on the marker where the Student Volunteer Movement was born. I have prayed there, more than once, at the grave of D. L. Moody, in the adjoining campus, asking God to use my life in the matter of revival in our day.

Young people can still be stirred. Moms and dads can still be stirred. College students can still be stirred. The problem is that we have become so addicted to the status quo that nothing really moves us.

The inscription on the monument in Northfield reads:

> Here, in July 1886, to the glory of God and the advancement of His kingdom, D.L. Moody and the Inter-collegiate Young Men's Christian Association of the United States and Canada called together a conference of students from twenty-seven states and many lands beyond the seas for the spiritual impulse, here given. From that impulse, one hundred men offered their lives for foreign mission service. A work of spiritual awakening was begun in the colleges. Similar conferences were established throughout the world. The Student Volunteer Movement was founded in 1888 and guidance was given to the Christian Student Movement through the years. 'I am the way, the truth, and the life,' so says the Lord Jesus Christ.

One hundred men said that day, "We will go anywhere God wants us to go to tell the story of Jesus Christ." Two and one-half years later that one hundred had grown to two thousand five hundred, five hundred of whom were women. In a few short years, over ten thousand Americans were actually on the mission fields because someone had a revival.

When we come to Habakkuk, chapter three, we see Habakkuk's heart cry for revival.

THE BURDEN FOR REVIVAL

The Bible says in Habakkuk 3:1, *"A prayer of Habakkuk the prophet upon Shigionoth."* This word, *"Shigionoth,"* means an expression of profound and strong emotion. It means that the prophet came with a heart so burdened and so broken that he could not go anywhere but to God. We must have what God and God alone can give. He prayed. The burden of revival must begin in prayer. We must pray and seek God's face. We must say, "We are turning to God."

I am no more disturbed with anyone than I am with myself. I am troubled because I am not as troubled as I should be. We must have a burden for revival. Many of us have talked about revival all of our lives, and we have heard preachers preaching about it all our lives. People talk about it everywhere we go. I believe that God wants to send it, and He will when we get a burden for God to do what only He can do.

THE BASIS OF REVIVAL

Verse two says, *"O LORD, I have heard thy speech, and was afraid."* A revival begins with God. The fear of God is a vital part of revival. Habakkuk said, "I was afraid." Speaking of sinful men, the Word of God says in Romans 3:18, *"There is no fear of God before their eyes."* There must be a fear of God. This is the basis for revival. There must be a stirring of our hearts about what is going on. As Habakkuk realized what was going to happen to his nation, his heart was stirred.

The Bible teaches that Jesus Christ is coming again. This is certain. And the Bible says that there is a day appointed for me to die if the Lord Jesus does not come soon. I do not know what day it is, but you have the same kind of appointment. My life on this earth will come to an end. I know this is true. If we ever intend to do anything for the Lord, we had better do it now. The basis for revival is God's people praying and calling on Him because they know His Word and they fear Him.

THE BLESSING OF REVIVAL

The prayer of Habakkuk is very revealing. He said, *"In the midst of the years make known; in wrath remember mercy."* He recognized that the wrath could not be removed. We cannot change the wrath, but in the midst of all the wrath, the Lord can remember mercy. This is the hope of the church. Our hope is that God will be merciful to us. This means, if He does not clean up everything in our town, He is still able to bless our ministries and help us be a blessing to others. In the midst of wrath He will remember mercy. This means that if the drug situation does get worse and if the public education system does continue to decline and if disease does run rampant across the world, in the midst of it all we can pray, "God, please remember mercy."

This is the blessing of revival. In the midst of all His wrath, God will remember mercy. This is revival–when God remembers mercy.

With Habakkuk, my heart cries out for revival.

*"When I heard, my belly trembled;
my lips quivered at the voice:
rottenness entered into my bones,
and I trembled in myself, that I
might rest in the day of trouble."*

Habakkuk 3:16

CHAPTER TWELVE

The Fear of the Lord

In Habakkuk chapter three, Habakkuk was still a troubled man; yet, God had spoken to him. Habakkuk's world was out of control, but God was still in control. God had proven to Habakkuk that He was the Lord of nature and of nations and that the reins of the universe were still in His hands. There are times in life when we feel that everything around us is out of control, but we must stop to realize that God is still in control. The Word of God says in Habakkuk 3:3-19,

> *God came from Teman, and the Holy One from mount Paran. Selah. His glory covered the heavens, and the earth was full of his praise. And his brightness was as the light; he had horns coming out of his hand: and there was the hiding of his power. Before him went the pestilence, and burning coals went forth at his feet. He stood, and measured the earth: he beheld, and drove*

asunder the nations; and the everlasting mountains were scattered, the perpetual hills did bow: his ways are everlasting. I saw the tents of Cushan in affliction: and the curtains of the land of Midian did tremble. Was the LORD displeased against the rivers? was thine anger against the rivers? was thy wrath against the sea, that thou didst ride upon thine horses and thy chariots of salvation? Thy bow was made quite naked, according to the oaths of the tribes, even thy word. Selah. Thou didst cleave the earth with rivers. The mountains saw thee, and they trembled: the overflowing of the water passed by: the deep uttered his voice, and lifted up his hands on high. The sun and moon stood still in their habitation: at the light of thine arrows they went, and at the shining of thy glittering spear. Thou didst march through the land in indignation, thou didst thresh the heathen in anger. Thou wentest forth for the salvation of thy people, even for salvation with thine anointed; thou woundedst the head out of the house of the wicked, by discovering the foundation unto the neck. Selah. Thou didst strike through with his staves the head of his villages: they came out as a whirlwind to scatter me: their rejoicing was as to devour the poor secretly. Thou didst walk through the sea with thine horses, through the heap of great waters. When I heard, my belly trembled; my lips quivered at the voice: rottenness entered into my bones, and I trembled in myself, that I might rest in the day of trouble: when he cometh up unto the people, he will invade them with his troops. Although the fig tree shall not blossom, neither shall fruit be in the vines; the labour of the olive shall fail, and the fields shall yield no meat; the flock shall be cut off from the fold, and there shall be no herd in the stalls: yet I will rejoice in the LORD, I will joy in the God of my salvation. The LORD

*God is my strength, and he will make my feet like hinds'
feet, and he will make me to walk upon mine high
places. To the chief singer on my stringed instruments.*

This is one of the beautiful Hebrew poems in the Bible. God, by
inspiration, delivered this message to Habakkuk. It is penned for us in
poetical form, preserved for all eternity in the Word of God. This
particular poem, in the closing part of
Habakkuk, is about God and His power. It is
about what God can do. Though all the world
is trembling in terror, God is still in control.

Notice what the Lord says to us in
Habakkuk 3:3, *"God came."* This prophet
was standing on the eve of the captivity of
his nation, seeking comfort, consolation,
help, and there was nothing he could do.
Have you ever been at the bedside of a loved
one, when the doctor comes in and says,
"There is nothing we can do. It's out of our
hands and out of yours"? Have you been to a
home where there is a severe problem and it
seems as if no one is willing to cooperate and there is nothing you can
do? Have you been so perplexed by things that you faced that you
thought in your heart, "What in the world am I going to do?" It seems
God brings us to situations in life where there is no solution. We come
to the place where Habakkuk came, where all we can do is wait for God
to intervene.

> *God had proven
> to Habakkuk that
> He was the Lord
> of nature and of
> nations and that
> the reins of the
> universe were
> still in His hands.*

The Bible says, *"God came."* When there is no answer and there is
no solution, the Lord comes down and meets our personal needs. The
Lord comes to us. He has already made the way so that He can come,
and He has promised in His Word that He will come.

Your life may seem out of control. There may be things that you think are
beyond your control happening to you. Remember that God is still in control.

LORD, SEND A REVIVAL

A science article in the *U.S.A. Today* stated, "Scientists believe the 6,500 plus pieces of debris now in orbit around the earth could hamper future space missions." They are fearful. They have satellite fragments, dead satellites, rocket bodies, satellite launch debris, and a few functioning satellites orbiting in space. They have identified over 6,500 pieces of space debris in orbit. Scientists now fear that if they send something else into space there will be a collision.

The Devil does all he can to convince men that they can control things, and with every attempt to control things and people, we simply get things more out of control. The Lord wants to bring us to our knees and help us to see that He is the only One who truly has control.

Notice carefully the sixteenth verse of the third chapter, as the prophet Habakkuk declares, *"When I heard, my belly trembled; my lips quivered at the voice: rottenness entered into my bones, and I trembled in myself."* This happened as he thought about God. Let us consider "The Fear of the Lord."

Remember that Habakkuk could almost hear the sound of horse's hooves from the Babylonian army coming to invade Judah. He knew that his land would be overtaken, and there was absolutely nothing that he could do about it. Judah would be carried captive to Babylon, and Jerusalem left in ruins.

Habakkuk needed encouragement. There was nothing he could do about the invading Babylonian army. It was out of his hands. How does one encourage himself in such a perplexing situation? Habakkuk thought about the Lord. He pondered on the subject of who God is and what God can do. When life is out of hand and we are sorely disappointed, never dreaming things would turn out the way they have, we should realize that God never changes.

Habakkuk said, "When I thought about God and all that God had done; my whole body trembled; my lips quivered as I thought about how I feared God, knowing God and what God can do."

God declares to us in Psalm 115:1-4,

> *Not unto us, O LORD, not unto us, but unto thy name give glory, for thy mercy, and for thy truth's sake. Wherefore should the heathen say, Where is now their God? But our God is in the heavens: he hath done whatsoever he hath pleased. Their idols are silver and gold, the work of men's hands.*

Speaking of their idols, God says in Psalm 115:5-15,

> *They have mouths, but they speak not: eyes have they, but they see not: they have ears, but they hear not: noses have they, but they smell not: they have hands, but they handle not: feet have they, but they walk not: neither speak they through their throat. They that make them are like unto them; so is every one that trusteth in them.*

In other words, their gods are no better than they are. Then the Lord goes on to say in verses nine and ten, *"O Israel, trust thou in the LORD; he is their help and their shield. O house of Aaron, trust in the LORD: he is their help and their shield. Ye that fear the LORD, trust in the LORD: he is their help and their shield."*

When there is no answer and there is no solution, the Lord comes down and meets our personal needs.

We do not know the full extent of what is going on in our world, but we do know something is going on. We are living in an age of confusion and fear. We need faith to know that God will take care of His own. We are to fear God, and when we fear God, we will know that God will take care of us.

In the book of Ecclesiastes, as the book closes, the conclusion concerning life is reached in the twelfth chapter and the thirteenth verse. The Bible says, *"Let us hear the conclusion of the whole matter: fear God, and keep his commandments: for this is the whole duty of man."* God says, "All of life is wrapped up in this simple statement: *'Fear God, and keep his commandments.'"* It is just that simple.

In Romans 3:18 God declares His conclusion about mankind, *"There is no fear of God before their eyes."*

If we believed what the Bible teaches, that God is who He says He is, and some day we shall stand before Him, then we would not behave the way we behave. The fear of God will change our behavior. Men would not laugh and scoff about how they treat others and what they say about God if they feared the Lord.

As we go back to the book of Habakkuk to that closing poem that God gives us, we need to deal with the portion of it that concludes in the sixteenth verse, *"When I heard, my belly trembled; my lips quivered at the voice: rottenness entered into my bones, and I trembled in myself."* When Habakkuk thought about all of this, He was filled with the fear of God.

Everyone needs the Lord Jesus. We do not meet anyone any day of our lives that does not need Jesus Christ. Little boys and girls need the Lord Jesus; young people need Jesus Christ; mamas and daddies need the Lord Jesus; senior citizens need the Lord Jesus; everybody needs the Lord Jesus. Many people are so very troubled and afraid. They are afraid of financial failure, afraid of disease, afraid of war, afraid of everything. But we must see from the Bible that God can give a calm and rest to those who fear Him. Fearing Him causes us to trust Him with our lives.

HE IS THE GOD OF MAJESTY

As Habakkuk spoke of God and the fear of the Lord, he pointed out to us in this poem that God is a God of majesty. There is not one like Him.

He is a God of majesty. As Habakkuk thought about the Lord, he said in verses three through five,

> *God came from Teman, and the Holy One from mount Paran. Selah. His glory covered the heavens, and the earth was full of his praise. And his brightness was as the light; he had horns coming out of his hand: and there was the hiding of his power. Before him went the pestilence, and burning coals went forth at his feet.*

Habakkuk was thinking about God coming to Mount Sinai where the Law was given to Moses. As we remember that story, we know that there was fire and smoke and that the earth trembled. The whole earth shook as God came. When Habakkuk thought about the majesty of God, he was overwhelmed. He thought, "There is no one like God. There is no one to be feared like God is to be feared. He is God; He is majestic."

In Isaiah 46:9 the Bible says, *"Remember the former things of old..."* This is a great admonition for all of us. This is what Habakkuk was doing; he was remembering the former things of old; he was remembering what God had done in the past. *"...for I am God, and there is none else; I am God, and there is none like me."* Friends, we have a place of safety, a place of refuge, a place of shelter; no harm can come to us. No harm can come to me unless God allows it. I am His and He is mine. As Habakkuk thought of God's majesty, he was filled with the fear of God.

HE IS THE GOD OF MIGHT

In Habakkuk 3:6 the Bible says, *"He stood, and measured the earth: he beheld, and drove asunder the nations; and the everlasting mountains were scattered, the perpetual hills did bow: his ways are everlasting."* Habakkuk was contemplating what God did when He made a way for His people from Egyptian bondage, led them through the wilderness, and helped them as they crossed over Jordan defeating their enemies. He was thinking about the might of God. God is almighty. No one can measure the earth except the Lord. Habakkuk imagined God, who made the earth, looking upon the earth and measuring the earth as a general measuring out a battle campaign. God sees exactly what needs to be done and He does it. He said in verses seven and eight,

> *I saw the tents of Cushan in affliction: and the curtains of the land of Midian did tremble. Was the LORD displeased against the rivers? was thine anger against the rivers? was thy wrath against the sea, that thou didst ride upon thine horses and thy chariots of salvation?*

Habakkuk knew that the God who parted the Red Sea and the Jordan and protected His people with a fiery pillar by night and a cloud by day is almighty. When we are alone and full of trouble, we need to look up.

The Bible says in verse nine, *"Thy bow was made quite naked, according to the oaths of the tribes, even thy word. Selah."* I love that word, *"Selah."* Three times it occurs here, and seventy-one times it occurs in the Psalms. It means to pause, to meditate and think upon God.

God's Word continues in verses nine through twelve, *"Thou didst cleave the earth with rivers. The mountains saw thee, and they trembled: the overflowing of the water passed by: the deep uttered his voice, and lifted up his hands on high."* When God's people marched through that Red Sea, the waters parted because they obeyed the voice of their Creator. *"The sun and the moon stood still in their habitation..."* Can you imagine that? The Bible declares the story to us of God causing the sun to stand still so the day would be prolonged in order for the battle to be won. *"...at the light of thine arrows they went, and at the shining of thy glittering spear. Thou didst march through the land in indignation, thou didst thresh the heathen in anger."* When Habakkuk thought about God he said, "My body trembles when I think that the Lord is the God of majesty and the God of might."

HE IS THE GOD OF MERCY

He is the God of mercy. Why does God do what He does? Because He is merciful to us, and He loves us.

The Bible says in Habakkuk 3:13-15,

> *Thou wentest forth for the salvation of thy people, even for salvation with thine anointed; thou woundedst the head out of the house of the wicked, by discovering the foundation unto the neck. Selah. Thou didst strike through with his staves the head of his villages: they came out as a whirlwind to scatter me: their rejoicing was as to devour the poor secretly. Thou didst walk through the sea with thine horses, through the heap of great waters.*

Our God is a God of mercy. It seems rather strange that we are to fear Him and yet, in fearing Him, we trust Him. There is no faith in God without fearing God. There is no trust in God without trembling before God. There is only one true and living God. I fear the true and living God. I trust Him because I tremble when I think of what God can do. He can do all things.

When Jesus Christ was upon this earth, He raised the dead. He healed the sick; He touched blinded eyes and made them see; He made lame legs leap for joy. He touched saddened hearts and made them glad again; He gave hope back to people. He is the only One who can give forgiveness of sin. When Habakkuk thought of Him, he thought, "He's the God of mercy." How merciful is our God!

He said in verse sixteen, *"When I heard, my belly trembled; my lips quivered at the voice: rottenness entered into my bones, and I trembled in myself..."* Then he said, *"...that I might rest in the day of trouble."* If we interpret this and apply it to our lives, we realize this is one of the greatest statements in the Word of God. He said, "In the midst of all this trouble, with my nation about to be destroyed; I've found a place of rest." Where is it? It is in the Lord.

There have been times when I have wondered how I could get through the day. But I had to remember that all things are possible with God.

Being frightened of everything and everyone only shields us from trusting God. We are not to fear things; we are to fear the Lord. When we fear the Lord, we will trust the God we fear to take care of us.

Habakkuk stood on the eve of captivity and said, "I can't change the hoards of Babylonians that are coming down upon us. I can't change the wicked desire of Nebuchadnezzar to take the land of Judah. I can't change the fact that the temple will be destroyed and God's people carried away; but I know that my God is a God of majesty, a God of might, and a God of mercy. I'm going to trust Him and rest in Him."

Let us trust Him today. Let us rest in Him today.

"*Yet I will rejoice in the* L<small>ORD</small>,
*I will joy in the God of my
salvation. The* L<small>ORD</small> *God is my
strength, and he will make my feet
like hinds' feet, and he will make
me to walk upon mine high places.*"

Habakkuk 3:18-19

CHAPTER THIRTEEN

Rejoicing in the Lord

W e have learned that the prophet Habakkuk was a burdened man. Judah was about to be taken captive by mighty Babylon. Later, God would deal with Babylon and a remnant of Jews would return to Jerusalem. But at this time, judgment was about to fall upon Judah and God would execute that judgment through the hands of the Babylonians.

Habakkuk called out to God and the Lord told him that nothing could keep this judgment from taking place. In light of what God revealed to Habakkuk, the prophet declared his praise to the Lord in the closing part of this Hebrew poem, when he said in chapter three, verses seventeen through nineteen,

> *Although the fig tree shall not blossom, neither shall fruit be in the vines; the labour of the olive shall fail, and the fields shall yield no meat; the flock shall be cut off from the fold, and there shall be no herd in the stalls, yet,*

I will rejoice in the LORD, I will joy in the God of my salvation. The LORD God is my strength, and he will make my feet like hinds' feet, and he will make me to walk upon mine high places. To the chief singer on my stringed instruments.

Notice what God said in the eighteenth verse of this third chapter when the prophet of God declared, *"Yet I will rejoice in the LORD."* I do not know of a statement in all the Bible that should bring greater joy to the Christian life than this statement Habakkuk made. God has designed our Christian lives so that when things do not go right, we can still be victorious. When the circumstances surrounding us do not turn out as we hoped they would; when everything we wanted to be made right is not made right; when wrong continues, we can still be victorious. *"Yet I will rejoice in the LORD."*

What is going to happen to your Christian faith when things do not work out the way you planned? God says that we can still be victorious. This is the marvelous thing about the way God has designed our faith. Our faith is in Jesus Christ, and we can still have the victory though things do not turn out the way we had hoped they would.

On a regular basis, I hear stories that are heart breaking. Christian people are suffering, and we wonder how they can continue. They continue by faith!

There is a story I heard long ago about a husband, his wife, and their little boy. The wife became very ill and died as a result of her illness. The day she was buried, the husband and the young son returned home. As the day wore on, the darkness came and bedtime approached. The little boy asked if he could sleep with his father. This was the day that his mother's body had been buried. The father granted him permission and they went into the room to sleep together that night. After they crawled into bed and turned out the lights, the little boy called out to his father, "Daddy, it's dark in here, and I'm lonely, and I miss Mama.

You don't have to turn the light on, but if you would turn over in the bed with your face toward me, I'd feel so much better."

The father said to his young son in the darkness of that room, "I'll do that." He turned over in the bed. Though the child could not see him, he knew that his father was looking at him. He was comforted and was able to sleep knowing that his father's face was turned toward him.

There are many times when we do not understand all that is going on around us. The darkness does not lift. The pain persists. But as long as we know that our heavenly Father is looking at us, that His eyes are upon us and that we are still in His care, we can make it through even the darkest of nights. We want His face turned toward us. This is what Habakkuk was saying, *"Yet I will rejoice in the LORD."* Let us learn to live in the *"yet."* Living in the *"yet"* is living in the presence of the Lord when the present surroundings are not what we wish them to be.

He continued in the closing verse of this chapter, *"The LORD God is my strength, and he will make my feet like hinds' feet."* He is speaking of an animal that is able to leap over barriers and obstacles. He says, "I'm going to be like that in my life. I have hinds' feet enabling me to leap over difficulties." He also says, *"He will make me to walk upon mine high places."* This means the Lord will lift me up where I can see from on high with better vision. Then the Word of God says, *"To the chief singer on my stringed instruments."* He gives us *"songs in the night"* (Job 35:10).

God wants us to fix our eyes, not on things beneath but on things above, Jesus Christ. The world is constantly trying to cause us to place our eyes on things beneath.

A number of years ago, there was much excitement about the so-called "Holy Shroud." This is supposedly the garment in which Christ was buried. I do not believe it is the garment that wrapped the body of Jesus Christ for a number of reasons, but the point is that so many people put their faith in that shroud and not in Christ. They try to prove with all types of carbon testing and dating methods that this is the

"Holy Shroud." I thought when I read all the information, "I do not need the shroud; I have the Savior."

We need to get our eyes on Jesus Christ. If we have the Person of Jesus Christ, He is enough. Habakkuk said, *"He is my joy; I rejoice in Him."* He said, *"He is my strength."* All through the Word of God we find this to be true.

Think back to the book of Exodus and the story of Moses after he led the children of Israel through the Red Sea and God brought them to the other side. In Exodus 15:1 the Word of God says, *"Then sang Moses and the children of Israel this song unto the LORD, and spake, saying, I will sing unto the LORD, for he hath triumphed gloriously: the horse and his rider hath he thrown into the sea."* Then we find this interesting statement in verse two, *"The LORD is my strength and song, and he is become my salvation: he is my God, and I will prepare him an habitation; my father's God, and I will exalt him."* He says that the Lord is his strength, his song, and his salvation.

> *"Yet I will rejoice in the Lord."* Let us learn to live in the *"yet."* Living in the *"yet"* is living in the presence of the Lord when the present surroundings are not what we wish them to be.

Notice what God says in Psalm 118:14, *"The LORD is my strength and song, and is become my salvation."* Think of that!

In Isaiah 12:2 the Bible says, *"Behold, God is my salvation; I will trust, and not be afraid: for the LORD JEHOVAH is my strength and my song; he also is become my salvation."* How does the Lord become our strength, our song, and our salvation? He becomes our strength when we are so weak that we know we cannot make it alone and we declare our dependence upon Him. We find when we are weak that He is strong. He becomes our song when we have done all the singing about the things of this world that we can do and there is no song left in us. All we have left is the Lord Jesus, and He becomes our song. When we need deliverance and help and there is no deliverance and help in anything or anyone else, we find that our only deliverance and our only help is in the Lord and He becomes our salvation. In the book of Habakkuk, chapter three, as the chapter concludes, Habakkuk saw that his help was gone; his nation was gone; his friends were gone, and his land was gone. Everything was gone but God! No wonder he said, *"Yet I will rejoice in the LORD." "The LORD is my strength and song, and is become my salvation"* (Psalm 118:14).

Do you know that the Lord Jesus is not as precious to us as He wants to be. He will never be until we see that He is really all we need. In the darkness of this world, when it seems as if things are out of control, my heart is comforted to know that God's face is turned toward me.

REJOICE BECAUSE HE IS ABLE

As we look at Habakkuk, chapter three, let us think about this statement, *"Yet I will rejoice in the LORD."* Why did Habakkuk rejoice in the Lord? He rejoiced in the Lord because God is able. He is able to do anything we need done. We cannot put a measuring rod on God. We cannot measure the depth or the width or the breadth of God. He is able! If we need Him for something, He is able. If we need Him for finances, He is able. If we need Him for forgiveness, He is able. If we need Him for comfort, He is able. If we need Him for strength, He is able. If we need Him for song, He is able. If we need Him for joy, He is able. I will rejoice in the Lord because He is able. Whatever the need, He is able to meet it.

When Habakkuk started out in this book, he cried, "Lord, iniquity looks as if it's prevailing and wrong is conquering over right. It looks as if the wicked are actually winning." There was an awful crisis in his land. He was under a tremendous burden. But, he moved from his crisis to Christ. He moved from a burden to a blessing. He took the journey all the way from his problems to the Person of Jesus Christ. What brought him there? He was dealing with such terrible difficulty. He knew that his land was about to be destroyed by this invading army.

Everything was gone but God and he found that when everything was gone, God was still there and God is enough. The Lord is able. Habakkuk was still rejoicing because God is able.

>
>
> *We cannot measure the depth or the width or the breadth of God. He is able! If we need Him for something, He is able.*

Let me give you a precious Bible verse found in Ephesians, chapter three, and verse twenty. This is a verse that all Christians should memorize. The Bible says, *"Now unto him that is able to do exceeding abundantly above all that we ask or think, according to the power that worketh in us."*

God says that He is able to do exceeding abundantly above all that we ask or think. If we are thinking about what we need today in our homes, with our children, with our jobs or with our sinful souls, God says that He is able to do even more than we can think. There are some of us who have big ideas about what we want to see accomplished. God says that He is able to do more than we can even think. I cannot think big enough to describe what God is able to do. He is able to do exceeding abundantly above what I think He can do.

Some dear Christian people think about what they can do to glorify God, how their businesses can glorify God, how their families can glorify God, and how they can give to the cause of Christ and serve the Lord. Remember, we have never dreamed a dream big enough to exhaust the ability of God to take care of it. I can rejoice in the Lord because He is able.

REJOICE BECAUSE HE IS AVAILABLE

It would be an awful thing if the Lord were able and not available. We are rejoicing because He is available.

When Habakkuk prayed, God answered. Habakkuk said, "I'm going up to the tower to watch and wait until the Lord answers." He was not simply speaking into the air. God was available. His message made it through to the Lord and God answered him. How I praise Him that He is available.

The Lord Jesus was not teasing us when He said, *"Come unto me, all ye that labour and are heavy laden, and I will give you rest"* (Matthew 11:28). The Lord was not teasing us when He said in Jeremiah 33:3, *"Call unto me, and I will answer thee, and shew thee great and mighty things, which thou knowest not."* The Lord was not teasing us when He said in Romans 10:13, *"For whosoever shall call upon the name of the Lord shall be saved."* If we draw nigh to Him, He will draw nigh to us. He is available. How I praise Him for that. He is available twenty-four hours a day. I can get through to God.

> *"Come unto me, all ye that labour and are heavy laden, and I will give you rest."*

Were you ever in an automobile accident and you needed God? Were you ever in an emergency and you needed Him? Were you ever in some frightening situation and you needed Him? Did something happen in your home and you needed Him? God in His great love and mercy is there. He is here. He is available. The Lord Jesus Christ went to the cross, paid our sin debt, and He is our way to the Father. *"Wherefore he is able also to save them to the uttermost that come unto God by him, seeing he ever liveth to make intercession for them"* (Hebrews 7:25).

Jesus Christ is nearer than our hands and feet, closer to us than our very breath, waiting to hear from us. I rejoice in the Lord because He is available. Let us live consciously in His presence.

There are many beautiful stories in the Bible about the availability of Christ, so let us look in the New Testament at one of them. In the Gospel According to Mark, we have a record of the woman with an issue of blood. For twelve long years she suffered. The Lord Jesus had been over in the land of Gadara. The Gadarene maniac had been saved. All of Gadara was frightened because of the wild man and Christ came to that Gadarene maniac and saved him. After his salvation, he was clothed and in his right mind.

Jesus Christ is nearer than our hands and feet, closer to us than our very breath, waiting to hear from us. Let us live consciously in His presence.

The demons were cast out of the man of Gadara, and they entered into pigs. The pigs ran violently over a cliff and drowned in the Sea of Galilee. Some of the people of Gadara became so angry with the Lord Jesus that they wanted Him out of their area. As Christ crossed over to the other side of Galilee, a man came running up to Him. The man's name was Jairus. He had a daughter who was twelve years old, and she was dying. He fell at the feet of the Savior seeking His help. People on the other side had just told the Lord Jesus, "We don't want You," but this man said, *"My little daughter lieth at the point of death: I pray thee, come and lay thy hands on her, that she may be healed; and she shall live"* (Mark 5:23). As a matter of fact, she actually died and the Lord Jesus raised her from the dead. Christ went with Him.

While He was on His way to the man's house, a woman who had been suffering for twelve years with an awful blood disease came through the crowd of people to the Lord Jesus and touched the hem of His garment. Do you remember that story? Jesus Christ stopped as people were thronging Him, and He asked who had touched Him. Of course He knew. He was calling attention to this miracle and He healed her. The Bible gives this story in Mark 5:25-34,

> *And a certain woman, which had an issue of blood twelve years, and had suffered many things of many physicians, and had spent all that she had, and was nothing bettered, but rather grew worse, when she had heard of Jesus, came in the press behind, and touched his garment. For she said, If I may touch but his clothes, I shall be whole. And straightway the fountain of her blood was dried up; and she felt in her body that she was healed of that plague. And Jesus, immediately knowing in himself that virtue had gone out of him, turned him about in the press, and said, Who touched my clothes? And his disciples said unto him, Thou seest the multitude thronging thee, and sayest thou, Who touched me? And he looked round about to see her that had done this thing. But the woman fearing and trembling, knowing what was done in her, came and fell down before him, and told him all the truth. And he said unto her, Daughter, thy faith hath made thee whole; go in peace, and be whole of thy plague.*

> *The Lord had a compassionate heart. He stopped because He was available.*

The Lord had a compassionate heart. He was told to leave Gadara. A Jewish leader came to Him and said, "Help my daughter." He was making His way through the crowd, weary, no doubt, from the work of the day. As He made His way through the crowd, right in the middle of it all a miracle took place. This woman came and touched His garment. The Lord Jesus had time for her. Do you know why? He stopped because He was available. He was available to someone who sought

Him through her need. I never cease to be amazed at how people ignore God. In the strength of life and the pride of life, they ignore Him. They say, "Things are going well; we don't need Him!" It also amazes me to know that when we do need Him, He makes Himself available. I rejoice in the Lord with Habakkuk because the Lord is able and because the Lord is available.

REJOICE BECAUSE THE LORD
IS ALWAYS THE SAME

The Lord Jesus never changes. He will meet your need and be there on time. Do not worry; He is always the same. If you think He is late, it is because you are early.

All through my life He has been available. Like so many others, there have been times in my life when I have said, "Oh God, how could this happen? Help me!" He heard me. He was there through one difficulty after another. *"Man that is born of a woman is of few days and full of trouble"* (Job 14:1). But He is always near. He is here.

So what do we do? We trust the Lord, and we rejoice because He is always the same. He is always there. When we call on Him, He will hear us.

Once I saw a special olympics race featuring the four hundred forty-yard dash. The young people who had special needs in mind and body had gathered for their special olympics. Perhaps you know someone or you have someone in your family who has been involved in such a thing. In the final four hundred forty-yard race, the special olympians were running and one young person was doing well, but he fell. He could have been first, but he fell. Unlike what would have happened in other races, the next two special olympians, as they were coming by, who could have finished first and second, did not run past their fallen friend; they stopped. One of them got under one of his arms and one of them got under his other arm and the three of them went to the finish line and all finished together.

As we go through this world, we see fallen people, hurting people, people with aching hearts. We are not to run on pass them as if they do not exist. We are to stop and tell them, "Listen, just a few miles back I was down on my face, but the Lord Jesus came to me and helped me and sent people to help me. Just a few steps back, I slipped and the Lord came to me and sent people to help me, and now He has sent me to help you."

We need to bear one another's burdens, *"and so fulfil the law of Christ"* (Galatians 6:2). Realize that all the dark clouds are never going to lift until the trumpet sounds and the Son of God comes and we see His face. Until that happens, we can still rejoice in the Person of Jesus Christ. *"Yet I will rejoice in the LORD."* He is able; He is personally available; and He is always the same. Bless His holy name. I will rejoice in the Lord. He is the God of my salvation.

Sunday School materials are available for use in
conjunction with *Lord, Send a Revival.*
For a complete listing of available materials from
Crown Publications, please call 1-877 At Crown
or write to: P.O. Box 159 ❖ Powell, TN ❖ 37849

Visit us on the Web at
www.FaithfortheFamily.com
"A Website for the Christian Family"

CROWN
PUBLICATIONS
Royal Reading

ABOUT THE AUTHOR

Clarence Sexton is the pastor of the Temple Baptist Church and founder of Crown College in Knoxville, Tennessee. He has written more than twenty books and booklets. He speaks in conferences throughout the United States and has conducted training sessions for pastors and Christian workers in several countries around the world. He and his wife, Evelyn, have been married for thirty-five years. They have two grown sons and six grandchildren. For more information about the ministry of Clarence Sexton, visit our website at www.FaithfortheFamily.com.

OTHER HELPFUL BOOKS BY CLARENCE SEXTON

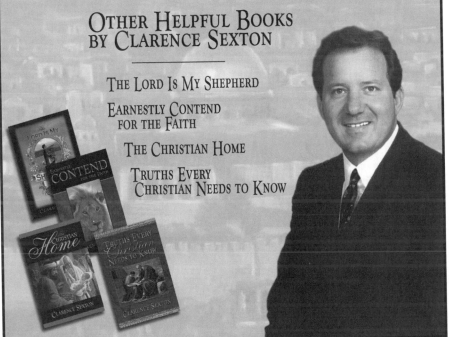

THE LORD IS MY SHEPHERD

EARNESTLY CONTEND FOR THE FAITH

THE CHRISTIAN HOME

TRUTHS EVERY CHRISTIAN NEEDS TO KNOW